First published in 2022

All rights reserved

The right of Janet Holben to be identified as the
Author of this work has been asserted in
accordance with the
Copyrights, Design and Patents Act 1988

Front/Back cover image Copyright 2022 Janet Holben
All Rights Reserved

Sentinel Publishing
www.thesentinelpublishing.co.uk

INTRODUCTION

EACH SATURDAY morning around 10.30 am, weather permitting, our small volunteer group meet up in front of the old Mortuary, exchanging news and gossip. A few minutes later we pull open the big double doors to choose our tools as we continue our prickly battle with the brambles and weeds covering so much of the cemetery.

But this account does not start at the old Mortuary – one thing the researchers amongst us now know is that in this cemetery of around 15,000 graves (27,000 people) there are stories of skulduggery and innocence, murder and bravery, grandeur and squalor – but mostly there are stories of everyday people living their lives.

This account will, I hope, bring some of those stories back to life and will perhaps bring an understanding of how Folkestone was shaped by terrible wars, widespread disease, the unforgiving sea, the new railway and fashionable society – but mostly, by the people who lived, loved, made their livelihood and finally died here.

DEDICATED

THIS BOOK is dedicated to the boys and girls buried in the old cemetery with no headstone or marker. I wish I could name every one of you – but these names represent you all: Lily **MOSS** (2 1/2), Clara **CHAPMAN** (21 mths), Arthur and William **BEER** (11 and 9), Phyllis **COOPER** (9), Dennis **HAYES** (2), Dorothy **JACKMAN** (14), Doris **WALTON** (16), Ethel **EALES** (17), Albert **CARE** (5 mths), Baby **BUXTON** (0). Phyllis **NEALE** (8 mths), Lillian **KNICHT** (0).

Throughout this book family names highlighted in **bold** font indicate that this person is buried in the old cemetery

~ ~ ~ ~ ~ ~ ~ ~ ~ ~ ~ ~

SNOWDROPS were planted around the old Mortuary building, and in other other areas, in memory of the stillborn babies which are buried in this place.

In the late 1900's if a baby was stillborn at 24 weeks or more they would often be buried in the foot of an open grave, if there was one, without any formal service or ceremony - and sometimes without the mother being aware where the baby was buried.

If there were no open graves these stillborn babies were buried in the small hedged area to the side of the Mortuary building.

These burials were not recorded and this small area had become forgotten and overgrown with brambles and weeds.

The 'Friends' Volunteer group with support from F&H district council are clearing and planting this area, as one of their projects during 2021/2.

When work is completed this area will become the 'White Garden' - an informal garden of remembrance so that grieving parents can visit this place if they wish to sit quietly.

THANKS

WHEN I DECIDED to write this book – I was surprised how happy it made me feel. Researching was pure joy – but I also had lots of researching help from my 'Friends' volunteer group. These guys are awesome in their support (and abilities) and I want to thank them here - especially Carole and Rob Moody, Karl Neve, Hugh Barker and Margaret Care.

Few projects can be complete without the support of your nearest and dearest – so I also thank my son Mathew Cooling and daughter Jenifer Lawford for their encouraging words – and thank you to my partner Richard Grundy who supported me in my endless walks around the cemetery whilst researching.

And finally a thank you to my late Dad James Edward Holben. My Dad died suddenly in 2008 - and like many father/child relationships in the early 1950's ours was not an emotionally close one - but I learned, after he died, that my Dad was a prolific writer. He never shared his writing with us, his daughters, or anyone else. But I like to think that he did influence me - and that me writing this, my first book, is more than just coincidence.

A mention here for my Mum, Marguerita (Rita) Edith Holben, who died towards the end of 2021. Mum suffered with schizophrenia the whole of her adult life. There is nothing to be thankful for about suffering caused by mental illness - but growing up in this environment did allow me to appreciate the invisible bonds and rituals that create 'family' and 'community' and I hope that appreciation is evident in this book too.

Image above: a frosty morning in the cemetery

INDEX

1. Where it Started — page 8
   - Folkestone Cemetery Plan — page 14
2. Everyday Life and Death — page 15
3. Smuggling and Other Professions — page 20
4. Religion, Fallen Women, Temperance and Skeletons — page 36
5. Tragedy Sacrifice and Courage — page 44
6. In Service Recognition — page 53
7. Titled and Eminent — page 61
8. Insanity and Mystery — page 69
9. Artistic and Creative — page 77
10. The End, or Is It? — Page 83

About FOFC — page 86
CWG plots — page 87
Air Raid plots — page 88 & 89
All other NAMED plots — page 90 & 91
Sources & Further Reading — page 92

CHAPTER 1
WHERE IT STARTED

THE STENCH CHIMNEY, which ventilated the smell of decaying corpses, is perhaps the first thing that gives us a clue to the purpose of the small building just in front of the railway line.

This stone building is where the corpses of Folkestone's poorer families would be brought before burial during the Victorian years. The bodies would be stored there on wooden slatted benches sometimes for more than a week, waiting for examination or autopsy, before burial.

Nowadays when a relative departs this life they are taken to a Chapel of Rest on the High Street where the body is prepared for burial, very respectful, and mostly out of sight of the grieving family.

However, during the Victorian years if you were a poor family you would not have been able to afford such a luxury and nor would you have had space in your overcrowded home to lay out the remains of your recently departed relative – so the Mortuary or Resting House was a place where corpses could be laid out before burial.

Inside the stone building up till recently it was bare, cold, dank and empty with an uneven worn brick floor and vines clinging tight to the old stonework outside, with creeping tendrils finding their way inside too.

Image above: the Mortuary or Resting House

There were no refrigeration units for hygienic storage of bodies to delay decomposition during warm weather, there was no drainage for bodily fluids. At the back of the old building, now walled off, are the slatted benches where the corpses were laid out. Inside the building you can see the remains of the Stench Chimney, used to ventilate the building of foul odours, going up through the wall at the back.

The Gothic arched windows now blocked up were once glazed with black glass so that morbidly curious passers by couldn't see inside.

With its newly concreted floor and small windows above the wooden door blocked off to stop pigeons roosting there – the building is now used for storage of out of date flyers and posters – and a selection of rakes, secateurs, shears and saws which our small volunteer 'Friends' group use.

Across the country, as with the old Folkestone cemetery, nature has taken over these old cemeteries and bunnies and badgers do their bit too - burrowing into the ground making it uneven and causing burial plots to sink and headstones to lean over at crazy angles.

Thankfully now, amidst this neglect we are beginning to wake up to how much recent local history is there and how these people shaped Folkestone into the place it was to become.

Burials in the Folkestone (Cheriton Road) cemetery span around 140 very eventful years including: the Crimean War and Indian Mutiny, rampant smuggling along the south east coast, the reign of Queen Victoria, King Edwards ascent to the throne, the Suffragists and the Temperance movements, the Great War, the deadly influenza pandemic of 1918, the Folkestone Air Raid and so much more – and there is evidence of all of these events in this cemetery – if you know what to look for. But first, an explanation of why and how the Folkestone cemetery came about.

During the Victorian years many new institutions came into being – the Garden cemetery being one such institution – asylums, the workhouse, public parks, prisons etc. being others.

Image below: Crows eat carrion, the flesh of the dead, so they have a world-wide association with death.

Superstition: Some believe that a crow near the house means an unlucky future, while others think it's a sure sign that someone in the house will die. To protect yourself during a crow sighting either bow to the crow or tip your hat to him, which should reduce your risk of disaster.

Corpses might remain in the house for between five and twelve days, partly determined by how closely the death occurred to a Sunday.

This new style of cemetery, as with the other institutions, was well regulated and with a defined structure but it was also unique in that it brought together aspects of landscape design, architecture, planting and social use.

As rural church graveyards, regarded as being inefficient and unsanitary, were quickly being filled the numbers of Garden cemeteries across the country increased significantly.

These new Garden cemeteries, sometimes paid for by private companies or individuals and in later years by public authorities, provided a place to bury the dead which met the social and sanitary needs of the community.

Garden cemeteries were designed with a network of pathways leading to chapels and burial plots – they were considered a dignified and efficient use of the land and became a place where one could walk in a rural or countryside-like setting.

Image below: An imposing memorial in the old cemetery

They were mostly divided into sections for the various denominations and were a place where all classes of people would be buried – but also a place where one could meet and chat with relatives and friends socially.

Back in 1855 her Majesty' Inspector R.D. Grainger Esq. came to Folkestone and advised that Folkestone needed a new burial ground because the new burial board had instructed the church wardens that no new burials should take place in the ground of their respective churches after 1st September 1857.

It was recommended that the new burial ground should be sited on loose sandy soil, east, north east or north of the town – the Cheriton Road cemetery (often referred to as the old Folkestone cemetery) has approximately 15,000 burial plots in it, with the first burial being in 1856.

This cemetery is now closed with no new burials having taken place since 1995 – although ashes are still interred in family graves there.

Looking at pictures of Victorian cemeteries across the country one can see that many, especially in the bigger cities, were sensitively designed often taking account of the geography and topography of the land.

As with many smaller towns, the design of Folkestone cemetery was a comparatively modest affair – an oblong shape, laid out with 30 fairly equal sized oblong sections. Along the back edge of the cemetery runs the railway line, with the main centre gate and side gate on the front edge accessed from Cheriton Road.

Looking in through the main centre gate towards the railway lines at the back - one can see the old Mortuary or Resting House. This small building was used to store bodies before they were buried, the old slatted benches at the back of the building where the bodies were laid out are still there, although this space is now bricked up.

Image above: view from the east towards the big pine in the centre.

Autopsies, if necessary, would be carried out in this building, and towards the back of the inner room, you can still see the remains of the 'stench chimney'– so called because it ventilated the room and allowed the foul air and stench of decay to be carried away on the breezes.

All sections to the right of the centre gates (the Cheriton end) are Consecrated plots. Sections to the immediate left of the centre gate are Unconsecrated plots – and to the far left (the Folkestone end) there are three more consecrated sections.

Gravestones mark a burial site. They often incorporate symbolism (such as cherubs) and euphemisms (e.g. 'now sweetly sleep') into their decoration.

There are pathways between the sections, not very wide pathways – but wide enough to accommodate the

Superstition; People once believed that when someone dies, a crow carries their soul to the land of the dead. But sometimes something so terrible had happened that the soul carries an awful sadness with it which prevents it from resting. If this happens the crow can bring the soul back to put the wrongs right.

Image below: Hugh Jan, Pat and Karl clearing grass and weeds from a pathway.

horse-drawn funeral carriages that were used at that time, also wide enough for a truck hearse which was pulled by men rather than horses and used for less grand funerals. Some of these pathways are grassed over now due to infrequent use.

The main entrance gate was the 'grand entrance' and there were chapels and a belfry there, although sadly those buildings are no longer there.

As you walk through the iron gates you can see the Machine Gun Corp memorial where Veterans and Civic Dignitaries lay poppy wreaths each Armistice Day.

Walking past the Machine Gun Corps memorial to the big Pine tree in the centre of the cemetery – and looking towards the Cheriton end there is almost clear line of sight to the Cross of Sacrifice at the far end - indicating that there are more than 40 commonwealth war graves in this cemetery, in fact there are 44 CWGs plus 3 V.Cs.

There is a shoulder height stone wall around three sides of the cemetery perimeter and wire and hedge fencing along the railway bank edge. Over the years, as families have died or left the area, the cemetery has been forgotten and neglected allowing buddleia, brambles and ivy to run riot there.

More recently the cemetery is tended by a small Volunteer group (Friends of old Folkestone cemetery) supported by Folkestone & Hythe District Council and in partnership they are gradually bringing this cemetery back into order.

The centre sections of the cemetery includes many of the bigger and more elaborate memorials, some of which have a vault or catacombs beneath for family burials, accessed by a flight of steps concealed under a flagstone.

These extravagant memorials would have been created for families of some standing who could afford it. The vaults were elaborate masonry structures within a plot, often divided vertically into smaller cells for each family coffin – each cell may be sealed by brickwork or a flat stone.

Tradition: White represents death, mourning, funerals, sadness, purity, and age. Black represents mystery and evil. Purple represents sorrow and mourning. Gray represents the elderly.

Headstones or memorials throughout the cemetery often feature beautiful and intricate carvings - sometimes indicating the profession or occupation of the deceased as well as symbolism of death.

Perhaps you are one of those people who occasionally wanders round old cemeteries maybe on route to the shops or when attending a wedding or christening.

And if you stop for a few seconds to quietly read the name on a headstone or memorial – you may wonder what the headstone tells you about that person; what did he or she do for a living back then or why did that person die so young?

Image below: Small stone tokens of childhood are often placed on the graves of children.

Sadly time and weather has eroded engraved lettering on some of the headstones, especially those headstones made of a softer material such as sandstone.

Some of the more grand headstones made of marble or granite have weathered better – but still there may be little information telling you about this or that person.

Perhaps as you wander around the old Folkestone cemetery I can act as your guide and walk beside you - and as we walk I can share some of these cemetery stories with you.

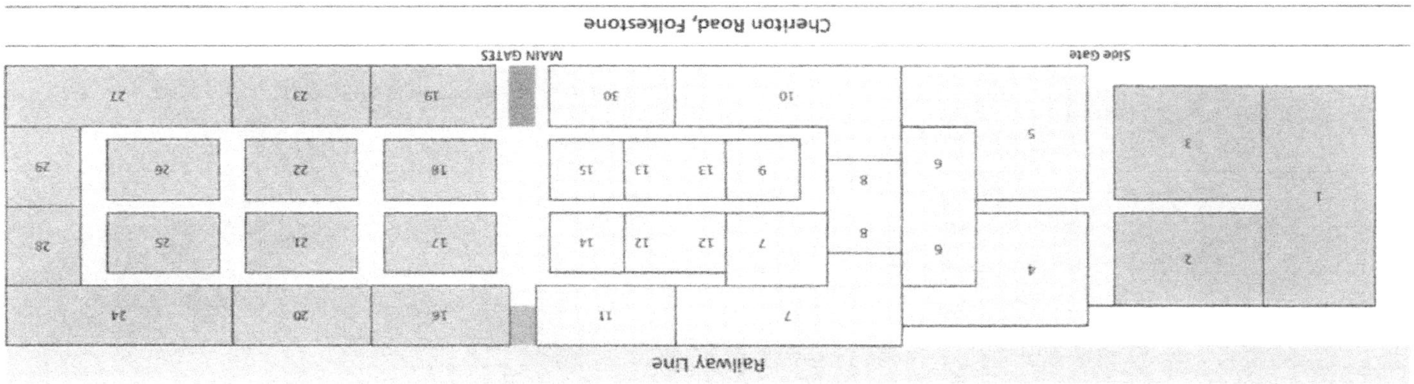

Folkestone Cemetery Plan

Dark Grey sections = Consecrated
Light Grey sections = Unconsecrated

CHAPTER 2
EVERYDAY LIFE AND DEATH

THE FIRST: It makes sense to start with the first person who was buried in the old cemetery – and strangely that person, James Paine **CLARK**, who died age 24 years old in Regents Park Collage, London on 28th November 1856, was originally buried in the parish of Mary-le-Bone (miss spelt in official documentation, but most likely Marylebone).

Shortly after that James **CLARK** was removed from Mary-le-Bone and interred within, what was then, the new Folkestone cemetery where his relatives are also buried.

THE STRANGLER: In the late 1800's the mortality rate of children was significantly high – mostly due to impoverished living conditions with little or no proper sanitation – and childhood illnesses were no respecter of wealth or title.

A survey undertaken in 1875 found that Folkestone ranked 30th out of 37 seaside towns for deaths - with 23 deaths per 1000 all causes - and 3.5 per 1000 for acute infectious diseases. Amongst the many childhood illness prevalent at the time were Scarlatina (scarlet fever), Whooping cough, Typhoid fever and Diphtheria – also known as 'The Strangling Angel of children'.

This characterisation of Diphtheria as 'The Strangler' was due to the way the illness developed causing a thick mucus to coat the throat making it difficult to breath. It was also known as the 'Kiss of Death' because it could be transmitted by a Parent (who was a carrier) kissing their child.

As you walk round the old cemetery you will see many headstones to small children some who may have died due to one of the childhood illnesses or perhaps shortly after birth.

The expression 'saved by the bell' is said to have come from occasions when a deceased was buried with a rope in their hand attached to a bell outside the grave. If the person in the coffin found themselves to be alive they could ring the bell for help. There were even coffins set up with tubes and mirrors so that gravediggers could peer into the coffin and look for movement.

Image above: Symbolism - Celtic Cross is a cross surrounded by a circle representing eternity or heaven and earth connected.

Image above: stone carving of an angel

A workhouse inmate could in theory discharge themselves at any time - although he could not just walk out of the door. He would have to give some notice so that his workhouse clothes could be returned (if not it would be considered stealing) - and he could be given his own clothes to wear.

Typical Sunday workhouse menu: Breakfast is Sheep's Head broth, Dinner is Beef, Pudding and Broth, Supper is whats left from dinner.

One small child who has no headstone is Lily Agnes **MOSS** – who died 15th January 1888 of Diphtheria, at the tender age of 2 years old.

Not much is known about Lily except she was the first born of parents Isaac William MOSS (tinsmith) and Elizabeth Kennison nee JELL. There is no marker for Lily's grave and, as was not uncommon in those days, there are two others buried in the same grassy plot, Clara 21 months and Lilian 32 years.

It is interesting to note that according to the official records Clara and Lily were buried within days of each other – they may have lived close to each other or perhaps being of similar age in life they were friends - or it may just have been purely a matter of convenience!

ENDS DAYS IN THE WORKHOUSE: Records from the Workhouse include details of an interesting Folkestone character – his name was Timothy **DALY** – and he was described as being a Rag and Bone Man or a General Hawker.

Timothy seems to have lived to the fine old age of ?? - well we might as well guess his age at death, one record has it as being 70, another has it as being 96 – and one account has it as being 101 although we do know the date of death is recorded as being 1907 and it confirms that he died in the Workhouse (also called the Poorhouse) known as Elham Union.

Timothy must have been an agile gentleman having the reputation of being able to kick a man's hat off his head even in his later years.

In those days records were not always accurate and it is quite possible that Timothy didn't know his true age and when asked by the Enumerator how old he was – he may have said any age that occurred to him.

Timothy was married to Mary, who may have been a few years older than Timothy, and Mary also died in the

Poorhouse and is buried close by. There is at least one child, Johanna, also in Folkestone cemetery, although records do not confirm exactly where.

The Elham Union Workhouse 1881 Census lists among its inmates: 2 blind people, 4 imbeciles and 1 idiot.

ELHAM UNION: Up to year 1601 it was laid down that each parish would be responsible for the maintenance of its own paupers – however, the Poor Law was overhauled during the years 1832/34.

During this overhaul questionnaires were sent out to more than 15,000 parishes, but very few parishes responded. To capture more information Commissioners were sent out to more thoroughly gather information and a report was compiled.

Image below: Masters House - Elham Union

The final report included the principle that conditions should never be easier in the Workhouse than it would be for those labourers who were outside it.

And if a man were to gain access to the Workhouse, then his family would also enter it with him, although once in the Workhouse men and women (and families) were separated.

The workhouse for Folkestone and area was Elham Union and the 1881 census lists more than 200 residents at that time, the oldest being Elizabeth a domestic worker who was 88 years, and the youngest being an infant of 2 months with mother 24 year old Jane whose occupation is listed as being a domestic servant.

Whole families would enter the Workhouse – as did six members of the Baker family, including 3 children the youngest 1 year old and 3 adults ages 20, 24 and 64 years old – but there were lone children too, their parents may have abandoned them or died leaving them as orphans.

Despite the basic conditions which existed in many work houses, inmates could live to a ripe old age. Records confirm that many lived into their seventies, eighties and nineties.

ALLEGED MANSLAUGHTER: The words on the headstone read *"In Loving Memory of William George*

Image below: Gravestone of William Holliday

Excerpt from 'Law Relating To Relief Of The Poor' - "Leaving aside cases of mental affliction and cases of dangerous infectious disease, it may be pointed out that no adult destitute person can be compelled to accept Poor Law Relief in the shape of an order for the 'Workhouse'.."

HOLLIDAY. Who in the morning of his life Was accidentally shot and died the following day August 26th 1885 Aged 13 years and 11 months" - but this epitaph does not tell the whole story about how this young boy was so tragically killed by a stray bullet.

The hearing as reported in The Whitstable Times and Herne Bay Herald said that; *"Charles Copping, on bail, was indicted for the manslaughter of William George HOLLIDAY, at Folkestone, on 25th August.*

Mr. Denman prosecuted, and Mr. Stephen defended the accused. David Foord deposed that he was the manager of Lacey's shooting saloon in Tontine Street, Folkestone.". The report goes on to say that the prisoner, Charles Copping, came to the shooting saloon at about one o'clock on 24th August and took some shots.

But when he cocked his rifle the third time, as he was about to fire a man passed by, perhaps distracting him, and as he turned round he brought the gun down to the 'charge' with the muzzle pointing down Tontine Street.

A Mr. Stephen said that he didn't hear the sound of the shot, although it generally made only a slight noise. James Standen, a Pork Butcher, who was carrying on business in Tontine Street, said that he knew the deceased boy William **HOLLIDAY** and on the 24th August his attention had been attracted to the shooting gallery, and he had seen the prisoner Charles Copping go inside.

Thomas Bottle, a Carter, living at Folkestone, said he had been going up Tontine Street on that day and when he had got opposite Messrs. Bridge's offices he had met the deceased William **HOLLIDAY,** who immediately proclaimed "I am shot" and Thomas Bottle had taken him into a yard close by where is saw the gunshot wound in the left side of the stomach.

Thomas Spicer, a labourer, said he saw the boy **HOLLIDAY** fall down, and on picking him up, he found he was shot. Supt. Taylor of the Folkestone police proceeded to apprehend the prisoner Charles Copping. After listening to the evidence the jury Acquitted the prisoner.

A workhouse provided: a place to live, food and clothes, a place to work and earn money, free medical care and free education for children and training for a job.

BOYS FATAL BRAVADO: Walk through the cemetery centre gate and bear left, walking towards section 5 which is just before the side gate. There you will find a typical gravestone to Herbert (Bertie) William **O'BRIEN** a 15 year old boy who died in 1909, and also to his mother Mary O'Brien who died just over a year later in 1910.

Bertie as he was known to his friends must have been an adventurous lad and on this occasion his adventurous nature caused him to have a terrible accident which killed him. A local paper reported *"It was shown at an inquest at Folkestone on Herbert O'BRIEN, aged 15, that he was killed through falling off a cliff.*

His brother, a boy of 13, said that a party of schoolboys went on the cliffs during the dinner hour on Friday to climb to some smugglers' caves in Folkestone Warren. Out of bravado deceased went higher, lost his footing and fell 300 ft".

The younger brother said he had found his brothers dead body at the foot of the cliffs. At the inquest a verdict of accidental death was returned.

It was reported that Herbert had been a popular boy and his funeral was very well attended. His funeral cortege was escorted by six pall bearers of the Army Ordnance Corp. and a representative of the 11th Hussars – as well as pupils and the Headmaster from St Marys Higher Grade School.

The Warren although a local beauty spot is dangerous in places. In 1938 the Fire Brigade were called to rescue three boys who had climbed up and were stranded unable to move in any direction – but saved on this occasion.

Image above: Gravestone of Herbert O'Brien - also Herberts mother who died the following year.

CHAPTER 3
SMUGGLING AND OTHER PROFESSIONS

Symbolism: Rocks at the base of the grave marker represent the 'Rock of Faith' – or the rock that Jesus built his church on.

WOOL TAX IMPOSED: The distance of crossing to be made, and the topography of the landing beach, often determined the nature of Smuggling or 'Free Trading' that local people engaged in.

Being within sight of the French coast, as Folkestone to Romney Marsh coastline is, 'Free Trading' crossings were undertaken in swift galleys and unloading would take place at the waters edge of a wide sloping beach – or more secretly at low points where cliffs edged the coastline.

Through the warmer summer months fishermen would mostly follow their normal trade of fishing – but come the winter months some would turn to 'Free Trading' or Smuggling to make their livelihood.

The smuggling trade was widely known about and is captured in this poem about Folkestone:

Image above: Clasped hands symbolises the relationship between the deceased and loved ones left behind and the re-union as the two meet again in the next life

A legend of Folkestone

Gay Folkestone, though now such a flourishing town, Was, forty years since, of but little renown; The ostensible trade of the small population, Was in fish, and their soles had a great reputation; But, besides catching fish, it was more than suspected, Other sources of lucre were far from neglected, And that many who seem'd merely fishing-smack skippers, Took a spell, now and then, in the fastest of clippers; But, whatever their traffic, it seem'd of a sort. That kept revenue cruisers from rotting in port.

W.H. Harrison (1868)

It is thought that smuggling wool (from Romney Marsh sheep) across the channel was how the smuggling trade started as far back as 1275 when the British Government imposed a tax on wool of £3 a bag.

The wool smugglers and in later years the 'Import' smugglers gained a reputation for savagery and there are many gory tales told of fierce clashes with Revenue Officers at sea and on land – but it wasn't only these confrontations that 'Free Traders' faced because the sea itself can be devastatingly fierce as every fisherman knows only too well.

This acceptance of danger by the fishermen and their wives is captured in lyrics from a popular folk song of the day *"Men must work and women must weep"* (the Three Fishers) which described the hardship of fishermen going to sea, risking their lives in storms to feed their families, with wives watching the weather and waiting at home for their men-folk to safely return.

FREE TRADING – A WAY OF LIFE: Walking through the centre cemetery gates and turning left at the big Pine tree in the centre you may come across an interesting memorial to William 'Cookie' **COOK**. The memorial stands about 6ft high, there is a big anchor with chain standing atop a headstone resembling a pile of rocks, with a preachers hat, and an open book at the front.

The anchor tells us that William hailed from a sea faring family, his father John Cook was said to be variously a brick maker or a fisherman during the summer months, and like many of his neighbours a smuggler during the winter months.

Following in the family tradition William was, like his father before him, a smuggler in his wild younger years, and in his older years he would tell the tale of how his father John

THIS POEM perhaps sums up the anger felt against taxation:
They've fixed the tax for the year today, God would never have done it this way, A tax when you die, A tax when you're born, A tax on the water, A tax on the dawn, A tax upon the gallows tree, Even a tax on being free.

Richard Lloyd

Image below: Memorial to William 'Cookie' Cook.

The smugglers of Romney Marsh were called 'owlers' - perhaps because they smuggled at night - or maybe because they signalled to each other by hooting like owls - or was it just a corruption of the word 'wooler' a term used by those who processed wool?

Image above: symbolism - a lamb symbolises the lamb of God, sometimes indicates it is the grave of a child.

Symbolism: Angels praying often indicates religious devotions. Angel pointing towards Heaven with outstretched wings usually represent escorting the soul to Heaven.

Cook lost his life, with all his crew mates, when 'The Jane' was sank;

> "I can remember when my father started for his last voyage. I was then only six years old, and cried to go with him, as he was going out with his bag on his shoulder.
>
> He told me not to cry, and promised to bring me home 'a young Jane' But it appeared they fell in with a heavy gale of wind, and the cutter was knocked down.
>
> The fact was she was so heavily laden with tobacco and gin, that she was not able to encounter the gale, and down she went with all hands.
>
> The crew numbered 53, and every soul perished".

This terrible loss of life was not unusual and it is said that in that one year almost 200 children were left fatherless due to loss of life at sea.

William was a very special man - and in his later years William turned from smuggling, and instead was known as 'Old COOKIE the Preacher' (see chapter 4).

William **COOK** was also uncle to Stephen **COOK** Coxswain.

BORN DUTCH: Following a research trail for William Brice **WILLS** who sailed on the infamous 'Four Brothers' and who died Sept 1883 – it was interesting to note how Smugglers were able to avoid prosecution if caught smuggling by claiming to be Dutch.

Records tell us: "During earlier centuries it has been the practice of some Folkestoners to give birth to their children in the Netherlands. The effect of this was to give the children what we call today "duel citizenship". This could come in very handy if these individuals were later caught involved in smuggling activities.

In January 1823 a confrontation at sea occurred between the fishing lugger 'vre Brodiers' (Four Brothers) of Vlissingen, Netherlands (Flushing, Holland) and the British Revenue cutter The Badger.

Smugglers wore masks and other methods to conceal their identity from officials who in small towns may be next door neighbours.

The lugger, crewed by both Dutchmen and Englishmen from Folkestone was engaged in smuggling activities and following the clash with The Badger the crew were arrested and tried.

Once captured the Four Brothers crew was taken to Bow Street gaol in London - and were trialled for murder, expecting they would be hung.

Witnesses swore that All the crew were Dutchmen - the Jury deliberated for two hours and to every-ones surprise returned a verdict of 'Not Guilty' for all the prisoners – finding that the ship and cargo were wholly foreign property and that more than half the crew were foreigners. On their return to Folkestone church-bells rang out.

DOVER GAOL BREAKOUT: Just after the 'Four Brothers' incident there is another story told about 'Breaking Open Dover Gaol'.

A smuggling crew were captured and taken to Dover Gaol. They would not be trialled for a capital offence as it appeared they had offered no armed resistance - but if found guilty they would likely be press ganged to serve on a Navy man-of-war. Amongst these men was Stephen **WARMAN**, a renown Folkestone smuggler.

As soon as word got out about the captured crew which were mostly Folkestone and Sandgate men – a plan was hatched to free them.

Image above: Gravestone for Stephen Warman.

A body of men left Folkestone for Dover intending to knock a hole through the prison wall.

23

Such was the amount of excessive tax levied that smugglers were looked upon as public benefactors rather than as law breakers.

Symbolism: A Draped Urn is thought to symbolise immortality.

There was never any doubt that the plan would work – and local people travelled to Dover to watch the breakout, with horses made ready to get the prisoners away quickly.

Before the gaol authorities realised what was happening the men got to work, but the breakout attempt was soon discovered and the Mayor of Dover summoned assistance including soldiers from Dover Castle.

By the time the soldiers arrived all hell had broken loose with Dover men and women determined to help in the break out. The prisoners were quickly moved to another part of the gaol, and the mob throwing tiles and bricks all but demolished the building.

The Mayor tried to read the Riot Act but the women rushed up to the Mayor and tore the documents from his hands, and into fragments. The Lieutenant urged the officer in charge to order his men to fire into the crowd, but the officer declined to do so – the Mayor fearing for his life took refuge.

Meanwhile, whilst all this chaos was taking place the group of men had continued working and had freed the prisoners, Stephen **WARMAN** amongst them, who were then quickly taken to a nearby smithy where their manacles were removed.

Then with all speed they returned to Folkestone and Sandgate where they made their way to different hiding places.

Many smugglers died at sea either in storms or in fighting the revenue men - or they had Dutch names or alias names – so not surprisingly they are often difficult to trace.

Image above: Pulley blocks used to lift heavy loads (Folkestone Fishing Museum)

However Stephen **WARMAN** born in 1785, listed in the census as a pilot and mariner, was one of the crew imprisoned in Dover Gaol - he died age 77 at Beach Street, Folkestone in 1862 and is buried in this cemetery.

The last two verses of popular song of the time tells the tale of the Dover Gaol breakout;

"For bricks and tiles flew so fast, From every part you see, And these poor men from Dover gaol, They gained their liberty. And now they've gained their liberty, The long wide world to range, Long life to the Dover women, Likewise to the Folkestone men"

Symbolism: A Dove is a symbol of resurrection, innocence and peace.

Image below: Stephen Cook - Lifeboatman

COXSWAIN: Stephen **COOK** born 1855 – a mariner and grandson of John Cook, mariner and smuggler, came from a family of fishermen.

In 1893 he was part of the first Folkestone Lifeboat Crew and was Coxswain of the local lifeboat 'The Leslie' from 1897 to 1919.

During that time the lifeboat was launched 14 times and saved 19 lives – and Stephen was always ready to be called to duty, He figured prominently in the rescue of the crew of the fishing boat 'Good Intent' (of which Mr John Saunders was Master).

This little vessel and another from Eastbourne, named the 'Pride and Envy' were smashed to pieces one stormy night on the rocks. The crew of the 'Good Intent' were rescued, but those on board 'Pride and Envy' were drowned.

Local newspaper The Herald (October 8th 1904), referring to the part Stephen **COOK** took in the rescue reported:

"It was a moment that will long be remembered by all who lined the jetties as they peered into the stern of the lifeboat as she came within call. "Have they got the crews" but not a soul ventured to remark upon the result of the lifeboat's expedition.

Two minutes later and an excited fisherman shouted "ave you got 'm 'COOKIE" Back came

Symbolism: Angel blowing a trumpet signifies the Day of Judgement.

High quality carving was often executed on even modest stones and flowers and foliage were common subjects symbolising chastity, innocence or purity.

the reply from the coxswain. "We have got Jack Saunders." Another query. "And his crew?" was shouted in the darkness, and as readily came the answer "Yes!" This was the signal for a tremendous cheer from the crowd.

But no sooner had it died away than the coxswain of the lifeboat was asked, "What about the other boat?" In a mournful tone COOK replied "She's gone down." And when as though in fear a fisherman asked, "Have you got her crew?" the large crowds which had been listening to the conversation were awe–stricken by the reply "No, they have gone down too."

Stephen **COOK** died at 68 years old and his funeral was very well attended, with many dignitaries, fellow fishermen and of course his family in attendance. Stephen received four medals; Mercantile Marine for War service 1914-18, British War Medal, Silver Medal of the Lifeboat Institution and the medal of the French Society, Sauveteurs D.L.S.F.D.L.M. Ville de Paris.

Image below: Folkestone Harbour station signal box

RAILWAY BRINGS PROSPERITY AND A DUKE: During the late 1800's and early 1900's Folkestone was increasingly becoming the place to visit for many reasons.

And importantly, in 1843 the London to Folkestone railway opened making it easier to travel to Folkestone. The Duke of Wellington travelled to Folkestone by train in 1852 to visit his friend John Wilson Croker a politician and essayist.

And as Folkestone became increasingly more popular Royalty visited too - in 1874 Empress Eugenie visited General Hankey at Cliff House, in 1893 Prince and Princess Louis of Batterberg visited, staying in Sandgate.

From 1901 until his death, King Edward and his friends (including Alice

Kepple the Kings mistress) were frequent visitors to Folkestone – staying at The Grand Hotel.

Image below: Memorial for Sir Alfred Watkin

These years also saw many literary figures visiting the area - H.G. Wells stayed at Sandgate for some years recovering from poor health – and many of his literary friends would also visit; Bernard Shaw, Hilaire Belloc and George Gissing amongst many others.

During these years the population of Folkestone grew quickly, the 1851 census recorded a population of almost 7000 - and in the following 50 years the population grew to almost 19,000 - and as the population increased so too Folkestone businesses grew and prospered.

As in life, the cemetery represents all professions although gravestones do not always include information about the profession of the deceased – but whilst clearing scrubby weeds and brambles away we have discovered a range of professional people who visited or lived in Folkestone.

ENGINEER: Sir Alfred Mellor **WATKIN** 2nd Baronet, he was elected as a Liberal party politician for Great Grimsby at the 1877 election although didn't stand at the next election.

At 17 years old he was an apprentice in the locomotive department of the West Midland railway, the 1881 census shows him as a locomotive engineer living in Castle Hill avenue.

In 1891 the census lists him now as a railway administrator with 3 servants still in Castle Hill avenue. And the 1901 census shows him now as a "Director of (South Eastern) Railways".

In 1911 he now appears as "Sir" on the census and is living in Dunedin Lodge Cheriton Garden, (which is now Dunedin Court and flats) now with 5 servants. He lived in this house with his wife (Dame) Catherine Elizabeth Payne and during his life

Image below: The Tite family memorial

Sir Alfred **WATKIN** was a Deputy Lieutenant of Middlesex, a Justice of the Peace, and a Chevalier of the Order of Leopold of Belgium - he died at this house in 1914.

BANKERS, MAGISTRATES: This handsome **TITE** family memorial is dedicated to a number of **TITE** family members, Arthur **TITE** being one. Arthur was a bank manager for Rothschild & Son, in London. Looking then at his wife, on the same headstone, who was a wealthy lady (in 1898) who left her millions to a close relative who lived on The Leas.

NAVY DIVER: The headstone, weather worn and with surface damage, is engraved with the name Edward **BRICE** with the bracketed word (diver) inscribed under the name. Our research finds that Edward served in the Royal Navy and sailed on the 'Bacchante' Edward received the Burmah Medal for serving in the Third Burmese War.

H. M. CUSTOMS: Local newspapers of the day reported that Benjamin Taylor **HALL**, who was an Out-door Officer (supervising and collecting duty on cargo, etc.) working for H.M. Customs, was promoted to the role of Assistant Examining officer in 1868.

He lived in York Villas, Sandgate, but later moved to East Cliff Gardens, and retired on full pension, living to a fine old age of 91.

His headstone is a modest cushion type headstone set into the grass, but still very clear to read the details.

Superstition: During Victorian years it was not uncommon for a photographs to be taken of the deceased, especially babies and children. These photographs were called 'memento mori'

BRAKES MAN: William Hayward **HINKLEY** lived in Gladstone Road and was a Brakes-man attached to Folkestone Junction station although working between the Juction, Harbour and the Pier.

On a fateful day in June William died from injuries received in a crane accident whilst unloading fruit from a cargo boat *"Witness said Look out, Bill! Mind your back!"*

cautioning the deceased against the tail of the crane. The deceased seemed to hesitate for a moment, as if he did not quite understand the meaning of the words.

He went away, but it was too late, for the crane caught him before he could get clear of the stanchion.

It squeezed him across the chain of the stanchion. He walked a couple of steps and then lay down."

In Victorian times a common practice of grieving relatives would be to pose the deceased in a realistic domestic setting – and family would sometimes pose for portraits with the recently deceased.

PERMANENT WAY INSPECTOR: One of the people involved in bringing the railways to this area of Kent is Henry **BECKINGHAM**. Henry was a Permanent Way Inspector on the South Eastern Railway which was a railway company set up to construct a route from London to Dover.

A Permanent Way Inspector was responsible for inspecting the condition of the tracks to ensure they are kept in good condition. Henry was 64 years old when he died in 1895.

STATION MASTER: The South Eastern Railways was a significant employer in the late 1800's and during that time S.E.R employed William **MITCHELL**, who completed 28 years service, most of those years as Station Master at Folkestone Harbour & Junction stations.

William was clearly held in high regard by his employer S.E.R and local people as was indicated on the occasion of 21 years service when it was decided to present William with a 'Fitting Testimonial' to mark his services to the travelling public and many dignitaries and local people contributed to this cause.

The funds raised by public subscription went towards *"a handsome ormolu clock, a pair of ornaments, and a cheque for £305,"* which was presented to William **MITCHELL** by Rev. A. J. Palmer at a private event.

Image above: Headstone for Henry Beckingham

Grieving parents would sometimes create lifelike versions of their deceased infants.

GARDENER: A headstone still in very good condition is to George **PEDEN** (died in 1871), with later additions of Mary is widow and Edward his son.

The headstone bears a unique inscription - a testimony to the friendship he had with his employer at Enbrook;

*"George **PEDEN** Enbrook, Sandgate. This stone is erected by the Hon. Sir John Bligh. To mark the spot and to testify his regard for one who served him faithfully as gardener for twenty years".*

By all accounts George was a gardener of some repute entering into many gardening competitions and often winning awards for Baskets of greenhouse plants, Bouquets of Flowers, Cacti (3 varieties), Fuchsias and more.

Image above: Headstone for George Peden

HEADMASTER: In July 1921 the body of Head Master Folkestone Grammar School (now Harvey Grammar School) Major Harold Arthur **DENHAM** was found in undergrowth in White Post Woods, Paddlesworth.

The body was found by boys from the Grammar School who were searching for their Head Master who had earlier complained of the heat. The body was found to have self-inflicted bullet wounds to the head, his revolver was found beside his body. An inquest later arrived at a verdict of 'Suicide while temporarily insane'. Major **DENHAM** died age 43 years old, and before becoming a school master Major **DENHAM** had served with distinction in WW1 and had been twice wounded.

It was thought that Major **DENHAM** may have been suffering with what is now understood to be post traumatic stress disorder.

Superstition: During Victorian years if you saw yourself in the mirror of a house where someone had just died, some thought that you might also die.

Major **DENHAMS** grave is in the front corner of the cemetery (Cheriton end) as close to the grammar school as is possible - although whether by design or accident can only be guessed at.

MARINER: The writing on this headstone caught my eye and a little research told me that Robert William **WEATHERHEAD** was an interesting and perhaps quite competitive man (see also chapter 5). The words on his headstone say '*He was one of the famous rowers of the six oared galley 'Sultan'*.

Image below: Headstone for Robert Weatherhead

Being a mariner by trade it is no surprise to find that he was an excellent oarsman too and he entered into the Folkestone Regatta each year and was described by his peers as a 'celebrated rower'.

Although on one short trip from Dover his small boat was capsized by a sudden squall. Being a good swimmer he started to swim but with the wind blowing off the land he was soon in difficulties - thankfully on this occasion he was spotted by a youth on Shakespear's Cliff who raised the alarm.

Robert **WEATHERHEAD** died age 52, in 1898.

TOWN CRIER: Folkestone's Town Crier Mr John **ANDERSON** claimed to be 'The oldest Town Crier in England' (died in 1931) and was fondly known by local people as 'Chopper' **ANDERSON**, or just 'Chopper', he seems to have been a larger than life character.

A picture in a local paper shows him riding a donkey on the sands surrounded by local admirers - but perhaps this item from the Gloucester Echo (Aug 1912) sums up his sense of fun;

> "*Mr Chopper **ANDERSON**, the Town Crier of Folkestone, has won more than local fame by the way in which he has scored off Earl Radnor, who is the Lord of the Manor, and owns most of Folkestone, including several miles of foreshore, over all of which he exercises a rigid control.*

The cheapest coffin in the 1840's cost 3s 6d, which was a considerable amount to find for poor families given the average wage for the employed could be as low as 4s per week with many families being destitute and with no regular income.

31

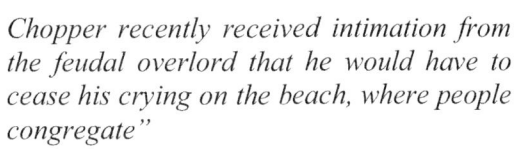

Chopper recently received intimation from the feudal overlord that he would have to cease his crying on the beach, where people congregate"

The news item went on to say;

"He is well known for the sharpness of his wits and soon evolved a scheme for getting even with the Lord of the Manor. On Tuesday morning therefore, contending that though his lordship may own the shingle washed up by the sea, he does not own any part of the ocean itself, appeared, to the great amusement of visitors, in a boat, armed with a megaphone, which was rowed along close inshore. Thus he carried out his scheme, and such was the magnitude of the megaphone and such the vigour of his efforts that his 'lost, stolen or strayed' could be plainly heard on the Leas promenade. Chopper's victory is now the talk of the town."

Image above: John 'Chopper' Anderson - Town Crier

Image above: Gravestone for John Anderson

WORKHOUSE MASTER & MATRON: Due to changes in the poor law between 1832 and 1834 the purpose of Workhouses (or Poorhouses) changed from being a place for 'aged and impotent people' who could not look after themselves - to become a place where the poor would be set to work – with each parish responsible for the maintenance of its own paupers.

All able bodied persons who sought poor relief were to be allowed to enter a workhouse – but they would have the understanding that conditions inside the workhouse would be more miserable than that of the poorest independent labourer outside.

After 1835 when the Elham Union Workhouse officially came into being it was overseen by an elected Board of Governors representing the towns and villages across Kent.

In 1865 the Poor Law Commission authorised spending to enlarge the existing building to accommodate up to 300 inmates.

The 1881 Census records more than 200 residents, 7 of these were staff including the Workhouse Master William **HORN** (died 1891), with his wife Ann **HORN** as Matron of the Workhouse.

Entering a workhouse was entirely by choice, it was not a prison where poor people were 'thrown'. Rather one entered the workhouse with a feeling of resignation.

The role of Master of the Workhouse included the running and administration of the Workhouse, although the role was sometimes compared with being a jailer.

It was not a well paid role, nor was there a career structure for advancement or opportunity for qualifications. The main qualification being that the wife of the Master should also be involved in the running of Workhouse, as Ann **HORN was,** in her role as Matron.

WESLEYAN MINISTER: Having just completed three years work in Richmond where he had also covered the parishes of Barnes and Mortlake the Reverend Ralph M. **SPOOR** came to Folkestone in September 1900 to serve as Superintendent of the Folkestone circuit.

He brought with him significant experience working in London and including three years service tending to the spiritual needs of the Wesleyan soldiers at Aldershot.

If an adult was to leave the work house - he would have to take his whole family, he would not be allowed to abandon his wife and children there.

Rev **SPOOR** earned the respect of everyone he worked with – being known for lending a sympathetic ear to those in need, never being judgemental.

It was 1904, Good Friday and Rev **SPOOR** had preached twice and was prepared to do the same on Easter Sunday.

Image above: Gravestone for William and Ann Horn.

Coins were a practical item to weigh down the eyelids of the deceased until rigor mortis set in —coins being round and fit in the eye sockets as well as being relatively heavy.

A large congregation was assembled and Rev **SPOOR** was preaching on the Resurrection – but his voice wavered a little and he became incoherent. The congregation realised something was wrong and church officials quickly carried Rev **SPOOR** into the vestry where he become unconscious.

A doctor in the congregation attended and everything possible was done – but Rev **SPOOR** died without regaining consciousness a few hours later.

Rev Ralph **SPOOR**s headstone bears the words;

"Whilst preaching at Grace Hill Chapel, Folkestone on Easter Sunday, the call suddenly came for the Higher Service".

Superstition: This practice dates back to the ancient Greeks who believed the dead would travel down to Hades and need to cross the River Styx in order to arrive in the afterlife. To cross over, they needed to pay the boat driver, Charon, so coins were placed over the eyes of the dead so they'd be able to pay the fare. Secondly, and more practically, many people die with their eyes open. This can be a creepy feeling, having the dead stare at you, and it was thought the dead might be eyeing someone to go with them.

Image above of Reverend Spoor as published with his obituary.

Image above; Grace Chapel

CHAPTER 4
RELIGION, FALLEN WOMEN, TEMPERANCE AND SKELETONS

THROUGH THE 1800'S and early 1900's Folkestone was, as with many coastal towns, growing from being a small place on the south east coast to becoming a popular seaside resort where affluent people would visit for the healthy sea air and sea bathing - which was perceived as being extremely good for 'nervous and bodily ills'.

And Folkestone was, of course, also becoming increasingly accessible due to the railway line being extended into Folkestone (1874). Through these years many events brought social changes across the country, and in Folkestone too.

The initial purchase of 229 acres of land by the War Dept. to establish Shorncliffe Camp in the very early 1800's, followed by the 1890 Barracks Act providing £170,000 from parliament (to reinforce the peace keeping and trading role of the Empire) saw Shorncliffe Camp significantly enlarged.

In 1830 the Beer Act came into being which meant that it was no longer necessary to have a license to sell malt beers – leading to an increase in outlets for drink and along with it an escalation in drunkenness and rowdy behaviour too.

This was followed in 1861 by the introduction of Grocers Licences which permitted shopkeepers as well as publicans to sell alcohol.

Drinking was now a way of life – beer was cheaper than bread, spirits were thought to have medicinal properties – and women too could now buy alcohol easily.

Image above: the dove is a symbol of resurrection, innocence and peace. If the dove is holding an olive branch, it symbolizes that the soul has reached divine peace in heaven.

By this time there were more than 80 public houses in Folkestone, many in the harbour and fish-market areas, with some hostelries being of extremely poor quality, renting rooms to drunks and prostitutes for as little as one penny.

Attracted by the prostitutes, soldiers from the army camp would flock into Folkestone, some using the hostelries which may have been used as brothels.

In 1847 the Band of Hope was formed to educate children about the danger of alcohol and in 1878 the Salvation Army was founded.

In those early years the Salvation Army felt justified in flooding an area with loud singing and clapping to save the souls of the working class. This would often lead to the 'Skeleton Army', made up of local men who did not appreciate the Salvation Army's self-righteous and forceful brand of Christianity, frequently clashing with the Salvationists.

Image below: A drawing of the skeleton army marching

A favourite tactic of the 'Skeletons' was to mock the Salvationists, they would parody the Salvation Army uniform, using dishcloths as flags, and they would sing obscene versions of Salvation Army songs back at the Salvationists.

These confrontations would often quickly become more violent as reported in January 1883:

> *"A collision has occurred between the Salvation Army and the 'Skeleton Army' at Folkestone. The latter had started on their march around the town, many of them with blackened faces, and others so dressed that their identity was completely obscured. Upon information having been given by their scouts that the Salvationists had also started*

Symbolism: A circle is never ended, so can signify eternity. Threes or triangles usually represent the holy trinity, the 3 nails to hold Christ to the cross of the Christian virtues of faith, hope and charity.

on the march, the 'Skeletons' commenced running so as to meet them.

Information regarding this intent was given to the Salvationist Captain (Peck), who ordered his followers to return to barracks at Bradstone Hall, but before they could do this the 'skeletons' charged downhill upon the Salvationists, the majority of whom managed to get into barracks but the Captain and Lieutenant Robinson were left to the mercy of the mob, who repeatedly hustled and knocked them about. But for the courageous conduct of the police the two men would have been trampled to death".

Image above: Symbolism - a cross is perhaps the most common and powerful symbol of Christianity - often carved into headstones or as this example makes up the entire marker.

REPORTS OF DRUNKENESS AND PROSTITUTION: With the 1830 Beer Act followed some years later by the introduction of the Grocers Act in 1861 the increase in drunkenness and disorderly behaviour grew out of all proportion. Reports in local papers about Intemperance and Inebriation were frequently posted.

Headlines blasted out:

> **Drunkenness** – *Edward J P was charged with being drunk and disorderly in the Fish Market,* **Inebriated Driver** – *Fredrick G was drunk in charge of a horse and carriage,* **Breaking Out Again** – *William S is charged with being drunk and disorderly in Tontine Street.*

And these headlines would often be accompanied with headlines about Soliciting and Prostitution:

Symbolism: A Calvary Cross - A Latin cross standing on three steps or blocks signifies faith, hope and charity (or love)

> **Well Deserved Punishment** – *Frederick F was charged with living wholly or partly on the earnings received from prostitution,* **Summoned** – *Lucy F was drunk in the Broadway, Sandgate, PC Reed said he saw the defendant helplessly drunk laying on the pavement - she appeared to be speechless,* **Conviction of a Sandgate Publican** –

> *Sidney E M convicted for permitting his premises to be used as a place of meeting for prostitutes.*

And perhaps more sobering headlines such as:

> ***A Drunken Womans Death*** *– which went on to tell of a wealthy widow who had given way to drinking – and was found by her horrified son partly undressed, lying on the bed perfectly rotten and with maggots crawling in and out of the flesh.*

Image below: Temperance poster warning of the dangers of alcohol

The changes in licensing laws making alcohol cheap and more easily available, Folkestones fast growing population in part due to new railway access and the increased number of soldiers in the area, as well as the growth of Temperance and Salvationist movements formed an often turbulent mix – but from this history of change and unrest significant characters emerged.

THE CHILDREN'S HORROR "DADDY" COMING HOME DRUNK

PLEDGED TOTAL ABSTINENCE: It is perhaps easy to see why the Temperance movements came to the fore over these years - and Sydney Cooper **WESTON** stood out for his Temperance work throughout the district - he had by example convinced many 'poor reclaimed drunkards' to sign the Total Abstinence pledge.

Many men and women had been led to the Fishermen's Bethel, a place to find a meal and listen to sermons, through his influence. Shortly after Sydney Cooper **WESTONS** death in 1893 a meeting was held attended by many local dignitaries to discuss a memorial to his name.

The Rev. Wakefield said that Mr **WESTON** was a most valuable worker in those practical days in what, to his mind, was one of the holiest causes – the great temperance cause in this country.

The funeral cortège comprised about 25 carriages – the ceremony was of the simple style customary with the Society of Friends, of which Sydney **WESTON** was a member. Up on Wear Bay Road stands a most handsome

Superstition: Birds were long held to be messengers to the afterlife because of their ability to soar through the air taking messages to the gods.

39

Image below: Old Cookie - a smuggler in his younger days - turned Preacher

cast iron water fountain commemorating Sydney Cooper **WESTON**.

SMUGGLER TURNED PREACHER. William **COOK** known affectionately as 'Old COOKIE' lived to be 72 years old and was well loved by all – he died in 1888. William was described as 'one of natures noblemen, equally liked by old and young, rich and poor'.

Being the son of John **COOK** a 'free trader' - for the early and wild part of 'Old COOKIES' life he was also involved in smuggling. However, he had lost family members, including his father John **COOK**, to smuggling and for the last 40 years of his life he turned towards the Temperance Movement.

COOKIE was a founder member of the Band of Hope of Folkestone – and involved in the religious instruction of the sea-farer. He was known as always willing to speak a kindly word - but he would also admonish in a straight forward way when he thought it was needed.

*"Every Sunday morning Old COOKIE had a certain round which he took for distributing pictorial card, leaflets, and little books, and the anticipation of this visit each week might have been seen by the children waiting at their respective doorsteps to greet Mr **COOK**, and to receive the little gift and cheery words of the kind old man – many of the children always clinging round him on his journey through the streets.*

On Sunday afternoons also it was an understood arrangement that at a certain hour "COOKIE" was to be found on the Dover Hill above Junction Station, where he was employed in distributing tracts and books to whoever passed in that direction, and it was an undoubted fact that he was most successful in winning his way and making his gifts acceptable even to the roughest he might chance to meet. In truth COOKIE was above all things a model tract distributor."

Old Cookies unique memorial includes elements of his seafaring background and his temperance work - a bible and an anchor.

FALLEN & FLEEING WOMEN: As Folkestone and the surrounding area witness a growth in public houses and other drinking establishments - there was also an increase in organisations and charitable groups, some supported by local nobility, set up to provide care for the 'body and soul'.

Superstition: there are a number of myths about birds such as hearing an owl hoot your name, ravens and crows circling your house, striking your window, entering your house, or sitting on your sill looking in

The Salvation Army provided shelters for homeless people, running soup kitchens and provided rescue homes for women fleeing domestic violence or prostitution, and there were other organisations doing this work too.

Amongst these organisations are the Clewer Nuns. At the Folkestone end of the cemetery the graves of **Sister Emma and Sister Marian** can be found, and close by is the grave of Harriett **MONSELL** (born 1812, died 1883).

Harriet **MONSELL** was the Mother Superior and **Ethelreda** was one of the barely distinguishable names also etched into this memorial.

These Nuns belonged to the Community of St John the Baptist, an Anglican order, also known as the Clewer Nuns, founded in 1852 by Harriet **MONSELL**.

The purpose of the order was to help marginalised women – mainly single mothers, the homeless and sex trade workers – by providing them shelter and teaching them a trade. The work of the Sisters grew to include working in orphanages, schools, convalescent hospitals, soup kitchens, and women's hostels.

In 1881 Harriet and Ethelreda were living near the corner of Sandgate Road and The Bayle, with a cook and a ladies maid. The Sisters ran the St. Andrew' Nursing Home in the Durlocks for many years. **Ethelreda** was a daughter of

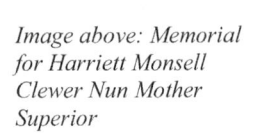

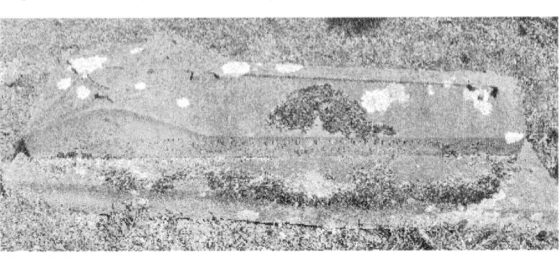

Image above: Memorial for Harriett Monsell Clewer Nun Mother Superior

41

You may not have noticed, but most cemeteries are laid out on an east-west grid with the headstones on the west and the feet pointing east. This comes from the belief that the dead should be able to see the new world rising in the east, as with the sun. It's also the primary reason that people are buried on their backs and not bundled in the fetal position like before they were born.

Image below: Headstone for Charlie Joy - Drummer Boy

Lord Charles Spencer-Churchill and Lady Etheldreda Catherine Benett, and was a granddaughter of George, the V Duke of Marlborough and distant cousin of Winston Spencer Churchill.

A third grave, on the other side of Harriet **MONSELL**, was Arthur **DAWSON**, a priest – it seems likely due to the proximity of his grave that the Priest and the Nuns were connected in some way.

FOUNDER OF BAND. The worse cases of violence involving the Salvation Army and Skeleton Armies come to a head in the late 1880's - after this the Army adopted a less confrontational strategy, and this change meant that most local people no longer supported Skeleton Army tactics.

Thomas Ingram **RAMELL** who came to Folkestone at age 10 with his uncle, joined the family coach-building business in Dover Road. Thomas became interested in the work of the Salvation Army and perhaps would have witnessed or even been part of the confrontational years – however he joined the Folkestone Corp. doing his best to promote their good work.

Thomas **RAMELL** with his love of music founded the Salvation Army band in Folkestone and was the band master for 21 years, he also played solo cornet.

He was very well respected and loved by Salvationists and had many friends. On his death at 60 years old an impressive ceremony was held, and he was given full Salvation Army honours. Many people lined the route to watch the funeral procession. The coffin was of polished elm with brass fittings and was covered in floral tributes, also his cap and cornet were placed on top.

THE DRUMMER BOY: There is a small headstone in section 8 which bears the once blue but now darkened and weathered grey colour Salvation Army crest – the headstone is to Charlie **JOY** a young lad of 16 years old (died 1890), referred to on the headstone as a Salvation Army Drummer Boy. Charlie **JOY** joined the 'Little Soldiers' Drum and Fife band mockingly call the 'squeak and thunder band' by the towns youth. Charlie died from a blow to the back of his head given by a 'cowardly lout' The headstone should have borne the motto 'Blood and Fire' which was part of the Army's crest but this was forbidden by the towns authorities.

Superstition: Another popular superstition is that you must hold your breath while passing a graveyard to prevent drawing in a restless spirit that's trying to re-enter the physical world.

THE MUD MARCH: One of the first women doctors in the UK, and a campaigner for women's rights Edith **PECHEY** became one of the 'Edinburgh Seven' - the first seven female undergraduate students at any British University, and proved her academic ability by achieving the top grade in the Chemistry exam in her first year of study thereby making her eligible to receive a Hope Scholarship.

To appreciate how unusual it was for women in those days to achieve the professional qualification required to practice as a doctor it is worth considering Edith **PECHEYS** own words in June 1906 when giving a speech to an audience at the London School of Medicine prize giving Dr Edith **PECHEY** said:

"When next you hear of a clever operation or diagnosis by a woman doctor, remember that in politics women are classed with lunatics and criminals".

Edith was at the forefront of the 'United Procession of Women' - known as the 'Mud March' which went under the suffragists colours of red, green and white.

'The Mud March', was a peaceful demonstration through the rain soaked streets of London on 9 February 1907, organised by the National Union of Women's Suffrage Societies. The march attracted more than three thousand women (no mean feat before social media existed) who marched from Hyde Park Corner to the Strand in support of women's suffrage - Edith **PECHEY** died April 1908.

Image above: Poster advertising the demonstration known as the Mud March

CHAPTER 5

TRAGEDY, SACRIFICE AND COURAGE

Superstition: The robin (image below) is thought to be a divine bird and also called spring birds because they symbolise renewal and new birth. If the robin flies into your life, it will teach you many things.

IRONCLAD GOES DOWN IN MINUTES: During exercises on her maiden voyage, off Folkestone on 31 May 1878, a squadron of German navy ships was sailing in two columns destined for Plymouth, with the flagship SMS Koenig Wilhelm and SMS Preussen in one division and SMS **GROSSER KURFURST** making up the other.

As they sailed under the cliffs, two smaller sailing craft crossed the bows of the German ships, provoking both Koenig Wilhelm and **GROSSER KURFURST** to make emergency manoeuvres.

The larger Koenig Wilhelm tore into the side of her companion ship spilling sailors into the sea, ripping off armoured plating and tearing large holes into **GROSSER KURFURST**.

The damage was fatal, and the ship rapidly began to sink. Numerous rescue craft urgently launched from Sandgate and Folkestone to assist the German sister ships in pulling as many sailors from the wreck as they could.

Despite this enormous effort, 284 of her crew drowned (the bodies recovered were buried around the memorial). This terrible news was widely reported across the country – excerpts from The Bristol Mercury read:

> *"The Captain also went down, but came up again, and hence arose the mistake that he had been drowned. The officer of the watch was drowned. A dreadful fate befell some 30 unfortunate sailors who, in spite of the commands and entreaties of the boatswain, who was standing in the forecastle, threw themselves over the bows and endeavoured to swim away.*

Myths and legends say robins are a spirit animal and a symbol of passion and honour.

> "But the sinking ship was too fast for them and they were caught in the netting which is stretched under the jib-boom, and thus entangled, were carried down with the ship. .. ... .as the vessel sank the steam rushed up through the waves, and must have greatly contributed to the loss of life. The correct number of men who lost their lives is 284. The complement of the ship was 497, all told, of these 216 were picked up, but three have since died from exhaustion making the total number of the saved 213, considerably less than one half of the whole.".

The old cemetery seems to be a good habitat for a variety of common birds. Including - we have seen: Green woodpecker, Robin, Jackdaw (lots of these), Blackbird, Magpie, Wren, House martin, Chaffinch, Wood pigeon, Blackcap and Starlings a plenty.

FISHERMAN SAVED LIVES: Small boats were launched with all urgency from Folkestone, Sandgate and all along the coast up to Dungeness when the call went out that the ironclad **GROSSER KURFURST** had been badly holed and had gone down just off the coast of Folkestone on that inauspicious May day.

The ironclad took only minutes to go under the waves and countless numbers of her crew could be seen floundering in the sea, with many men being pulled under the waves by the slipstream or caught as they were in the netting which pulled them under despite attempts by the **KURFURSTS** sister-ships the SMS Koenig Wilhelm and SMS Preussen to save their compatriots.

Image below: Grosser Kurfurst - an ironclad turret ship on her maiden voyage (Wikipedia)

One of the brave local men who immediately rushed into action on that fateful day was William **SAUNDERS**, who was remembered as being one of the 'oldest fishermen', and listed in the 1861 census as a Mariner. William **SAUNDERS** was well known around the fish-market – credited as being one of the strongest men, if not *the* strongest, aboard the Folkestone luggers.

45

William had many seafaring tales to tell – one of these tales would be about the **GROSSER KURFURST**. William was credited with saving the lives of 15 sailors - putting himself in great danger. William **SAUNDERS** died age 89.

The **GROSSER KURFURST** memorial, with its splendid gold lettering, stands proud in an area surrounded by grass where more than 100 men were buried, side by side.

Later that same year the German Government presented awards to men from Folkestone to Dungeness for 'services rendered' in attempting to save lives and to recover bodies – a significant sum of money was to be divided amongst them, and their officers also received valuable gifts.

Image above: Imposing memorial to approximately more than 700 Grosser Kurfurst crew who are buried in the grassed area surrounding the memorial.

DAYLIGHT AIR RAID: There are several excellent accounts of the **FOLKESTONE AIR RAID** (also known as the Tontine Street Bombing or the Gotha Bombing) which happened on 25th May 1917 - so this account will not attempt to describe it at great length.

Except to say that this bombing raid caused the death on that day, or from injuries soon after, of almost 100 people - including many children:

> *"For ten minutes or so death literally rained from the sky— sky of azure blue—causing the streets in some parts of the town to run with blood, and carrying bleak desolation into scores of homes".*

Daylight Air Raid: "In that moment the street was filled with dead and dying, some torn limb from limb, intermingled with the human bodies were the lifeless and mangled carcases of horses."

John English

The bomb that hit Tontine Street was the tail end of an air raid which came across from Ashford over Hythe and Shorncliffe – but just one bomb dropped on Tontine street - and in that dreadful moment killed around 60 civilians – ordinary people, many mothers with children who were doing their shopping, queuing outside the green-grocers waiting to be served. An account of the event written shortly after said:

> *"truly it was a terrific awakening, horrifying, for a brief interval almost stupefying! If the town staggered and reeled under the blow — blow so utterly unexpected — perhaps it may be forgiven, for the raid was (up to that time) the biggest and most deadly raid of the War".*

Image below: Digging the graves after the May 25th 1917 air raid. Some of those buried in these graves were moved to family graves nearby shortly after.

News of the event was censored at the time as it would perhaps have caused widespread panic across the country. One local newspapers observed on 2nd June 1917:

> *"The first notice gave no indication of the towns attacked, and on Monday The Times remarked that even now there is a ridiculous ban on the name of the town where the bulk of the casualties occurred in the full light of day. We are now permitted to announce that the town is Folkestone"*

As you wander round the old cemetery, here and there, you may come across headstones which indicate the deceased was killed in the Air Raid.

A headstone for Annie **BEER** and her daughter Rosie **BEER** can be found in Section 2, consecrated, with brothers Stephen and William **BEER** (no headstone for the brothers) who were nephews of Annie **BEER**, also buried close by.

Also in Section 2 you find the headstone for Florence Louise, Florence Kathleen & William Alfred **NORRIS** (mother and children) - age 24 years old, 2 years old and 10 months old respectively – little William Alfred **NORRIS** being the youngest Air Raid victim buried in this cemetery.

Not all Air Raid victims have headstones – some families may have been at that time too poor to afford a headstone – but one can appreciate the devastation each family

A listing of Air Raid graves can be found on page 87

Image above: a plaque to commemorate the victims of the Gotha Bombing at the site of the bombing.

Cemeteries are good places for bats because there are often old trees. This cemetery is relatively new but it is possible that you may see pipistrelles feeding here.

would have felt at losing a family member, and in many instances more than one.

On 25th May 2017 a service was held to commemorate the Air Raid victims, with families of the victims and local dignitaries attending the service and afterwards to unveil a plaque in Christchurch Garden of Remembrance.

More information about the Folkestone Air Raid with names of victims buried in the old cemetery (also names of those killed but buried elsewhere) is also included on an Interpretation Panel which was installed Nov 2017 – sited in the old cemetery close to the main entrance gate.

An excellent and detailed account of this event can be found in a book titled 'Glint In The Sky'.

A RESCUER DROWNED: On a warm early summer evening local boys went swimming in a well known pond locals called the Black Pond at the Warren, a local beauty spot, when tragedy struck.

One boy, Arthur, became tangled and stuck in mud and weeds. Reporting on the local story The Dover Express wrote;

> *"When Arthur Waller, aged 15, of Bridge Street, Folkestone, got into difficulties while bathing in a pond at Folkestone Warren on Sunday night Albert (should be Herbert)* **COPPING***, aged 20 (he was 21), of Denmark Street, Folkestone, jumped into the water, caught hold of the boy who was stuck in mud, and brought him close to the bank where he was lifted out of the pond by other people.*
>
> *Herbert* **COPPING***, however, disappeared and another youth of about 19, who went into the pond, was unable to bring him above the water again, as he had become entangled in the weeds".*

The words on the modest headstone echo the parents pain at their loss but also their pride in Herbert their son – and reads:

> *"Greater love hath no man than this In proud and affectionate memory of our eldest son Herbert G M* **COPPING** *Aged 21 years. Who was drowned in the Warren Pond. After saving the life of a boy who was bathing on Sunday 19th July 1925. Old England can boast her satisfaction To have borne a son for such an action."*

Image above: Headstone for Herbert Copping,

BRAVE FISHERMEN: There are many instances of bravery by Folkestone fishermen, sometimes sadly leading to loss of life – and this is captured in an article published in the Nottingham Daily Express 1886:

> *"Press Opinions: The Times remarks that the gloomy predictions in the weather forecasts issued on Thursday have been more than verified by the event. The threatened gale has come, and has proved to be of a violence unsurpassed during many years. We have reports from all sides of disaster by land and sea. The Standard says that in the midst of so much destruction and disaster it is pleasant to find examples of the courage and heroism which such occasions never fail to produce"*

GREAT GALE OF 1886: One of the ships that suffered in the storm of 1886 was the Norwegian barque 'Ellida'. It was a stormy winter evening and the 'Ellida' had run onto rocks about three hundred yards outside the reef between Folkestone and Sandgate.

Superstition: if strange sounds were heard whilst at sea - it would often be blamed on sirens, or mermaids - who sang enchanted songs which lured sailors into dangerous waters where their ships could be dashed against the rocks.

Image above: a larger than life-size stone angel.

Superstition: In times past bees were believed to be the messengers of the gods, so when a member of the household dies you should go outside and whisper it to the bees - the bees would then take the news to the gods.

The coastguards had immediately set up rocket apparatus to the shore and the rockets were fired and despite the raging wind were well positioned to help save the crew.

Meanwhile six fishermen - Stephen **HALL**, Robert **WEATHERHEAD** (see also chapter 3), William **FRODSHAM**, John **HART**, Edward **FAGG** and William Henry **MARSHALL** had decided that they would try to drag the crew to safety through the surf and rocks and they looked for, and found, a coastguard boat and launched it. There were cork jackets on board but they decided these were too cumbersome and more likely to hinder or even drown them.

They navigated the coastguard boat between the rocks, through the roaring and breaking waves. It was pitch black with blinding rain and howling wind.

One of the men shouted against the noise of the waves: *"If we're drowned, we can only be drowned once".*

The fisherman crew carefully and skilfully made their way through the rocks and the 'Ellida' crew jumped into their boat, the captain being an older man had to be caught when he jumped. The six Folkestone fishermen with the 'Ellida' crew made it safely back to shore just before the Ellida started breaking up.

Records confirmed that all six of these brave fishermen are buried in the Folkestone cemetery.

This is but one example of Folkestone fishermen risking their lives to save the lives of others, there are many other stories.

CALAMITOUS STORM, 1891: The storms of 1891 battered the South-East coastline and caused devastation on land and sea. There was serious and extensive damage to rooftops with tiles and slates flying through the air, windows were smashed and damage caused to properties across Folkestone.

Anyone who was outside risked life and limb with many injuries being caused by hurricane winds – and there was loss of life at sea too.

Superstition: Some sailors have a fatalistic view of the sea and believe that "What the sea wants, the sea will have"

During this storm the fully rigged ship Benvenue, was on route to Sydney, when the Captain dropped anchor 400 to 500 yards off Sandgate to avoid being pushed in-shore by the winds.

This caused the ship to abruptly swing round with the hull hitting bottom causing the ship to sink quickly with the hull under several feet of water.

The captain and crew had climbed the mizzen mast for safety and were huddled there, some tied themselves to the mast for safety, for some hours whilst many attempts were made to save them.

With each attempt the hurricane winds and rough seas beat the lifeboats back, capsizing the Sandgate Lifeboat. With the Dungeness and Littlestone Lifeboats already engaged in rescue work further along the coast – it seemed to be an impossible task.

The 'Benvenue' crew, clinging to the mizzen mast were cold and soaked through, exhausted and getting weaker as the hours went by – they had seen five of their crew drowned and washed away by the sea - the Captain, two boy apprentices, the steward and a seaman.

The surviving crew clung to the mizzen mast for more than 15 hours as attempt after attempt was made to save them, finally a fresh volunteer crew were found to man the Sandgate Lifeboat which would try again.

The lifeboat crew was a 'scratch' crew made up of local fisherman and some coastguards; Lawrence HENNESSEY, Albert SADLER, John **CORRIE**, David

Image above: a drawing of the Benvenue crew clinging to the mast

Superstition: It is considered unlucky to set sail on a Friday.

PHILPOTT a mariner, Robert **WEATHERHEAD** a mariner (see also chapter 3), Robert **FREEMAN** a boatman, Thomas MOORE, Albert MOORE, Robert **FAGG** a fisherman, Thomas NEWMAN, Walter SMITH, Edward MEES, GRIGGS, Nicholas **WILLIAMS** a mariner and Thomas SHELLY.

Finally these brave men managed to get the 27 surviving crew into the lifeboat which by now was so overcrowded that some of the lifeboat crew stayed in the water clinging to lifelines for the homeward leg of the rescue.

Superstition: It was thoughts that birds carried the souls of dead sailors. Killing a gull or an albatross would bring bad luck.

Superstition: It was thought the tides had an effect on death - and if someone was badly ill or injured, death would come on the ebb tide.

Image above; The Benvenue - only her masts above water.

52

CHAPTER 6
IN SERVICE RECOGNITION

DIED IN SERVICE. If you find yourself keeping to the shade of trees on a warm summer day you may come across the memorial to Phyllis **DECK**.

Three square stones of reducing size placed on top of each other form the base of this memorial and atop the base was a stone cross - that cross now lies full length on the earth. Words carved into the stone base read:

*"Phyllis **DECK** Who Died In The Service Of Her King And Country".*

Phyllis, one of six daughters, was born in 1894 in the Wolverhampton District.

Her father Rev Deck brought his family to Folkestone to take up the position of vicar at Christchurch, the family lived at the Vicarage, 31 Cheriton Gardens and on his death moved to 15 Wiltie Gardens, Folkestone.

Image above; Memorial to Phyllis Deck.

In 1914 Phyllis **DECK** took up the role of probationer nurse at the Royal Victoria Hospital in Dover – she progressed and in 1917 achieved the rank of Staff Nurse. In January 1918, she moved again, this time to the Manor House Hospital, Folkestone – now as Nursing Sister.

Sadly Phyllis could not progress in her career further as she died of bronchitis and pleurisy following influenza, just 24 years old, at Manor House Hospital on 6th October 1918.

Nature: Snowdrops are known as the 'flower of hope' - being the first to flower after winter.

Phyllis was popular with her nursing colleagues - and the local paper reported:

53

Image below: the Machine Gun Corp memorial - close to the main entrance.

"amongst the wreaths sent was one from the hospital staff, another from the medical staff and one from the staff of the Royal Victoria Hospital, Dover. The deceased, who was 24 years age did much good work both in Dover and Folkestone".

The funeral service was held at St. John' Church followed by a burial in Cheriton Road Cemetery, Folkestone.

Phyllis **DECK** is also commemorated on a tablet rescued from the debris of Christchurch which was partly destroyed by WW2 enemy action (the tablet was later moved to Holy Trinity Church, Folkestone).

A GREAT FIGHTING CORP: The MACHINE GUN CORP. memorial to the 497 members of the mounted section of the Cavalry Unit who died in WW1 stands just inside the main entrance gate.

The memorial was unveiled by Major General Sir F. H. Sykes in February 1921 and commemorates the Unit set up for the duration of the War only.

The Unit were disbanded in 1922, its last Headquarters was at nearby Shorncliffe Camp.

"No military pomp attended its birth or decease. It was not a famous regiment with glamour and whatnot, but a great fighting corps, born for war only and not for parades. From the moment of its formation it was kicking.

"It was with much sadness that I recall its disbandment in 1922; like old soldiers it simply faded away" so wrote former machine gunner George Coppard.

On Armistice Day each year Veterans and their families gather in the Folkestone cemetery around the **MACHINE GUN CORP.** memorial, along with local dignitaries, to commemorate the end of WW1.

THE HIGHEST AWARD – VICTORIA CROSS. The old cemetery has three recipients of the Victoria Cross (V.C) - Britain's highest award.

John Edmund COMMERELL V.C: Born in London, England, John Edmund **COMMERELL** served as a Commander in the Royal Navy. On October 11, 1855, in the Sea of Azov, Crimea, Commander **COMMERELL** was an officer of the ship HMS Weser, when he went with a Quartermaster and a Seaman to destroy large quantities of forage on the shore of the Sivash.

After a difficult and dangerous journey they reached their objective and managed to ignite the fodder stacks. The shore guards were alerted and immediately opened fire and gave chase. The pursuit was hot and although the three men were fatigue, they finally reached their ship and later the look-outs reported that the fodder store had burned to the ground. For most prestigious gallantry John Edmund **COMMERELL** was awarded the Victoria Cross on February 24, 1857.

Remaining in the Royal Navy, he later achieved the rank of Admiral Commander in Chief of the North America and West Indies Stations, retiring in 1891. He died at age 72 in Hyde Park, England and is buried in section 22 of Folkestone cemetery. (Bio by John "J-Cat" Griffith)

Image above: Memorial for John Commerell V.C.

Mark WALKER V.C: Born at Gore Port, Finea, in County Westmeath, **Mark WALKER** the son of a Captain in the British Army, he was educated at Arlington House in Portarlington, County Laois, and, in 1846, joined the 30th Foot Regiment. Over the next few years, he served in the Ionian Islands and in Gibraltar. In February 1854, he was promoted to the rank of Lieutenant; in May the same year, on the outbreak of the Crimean War, the regiment left for Scutari. On September 20, 1854, at the Battle of the Alma, **WALKER** had his horse shot from under him and

Image below: Memorial for Mark Walker V.C.

was wounded in the chest, but made the march to Balaklava and was present at its capture.

The following day, the advance was made to the Inkerman Heights. On November 5th, at the Battle of Inkerman, as two battalions of Russian infantry were approaching, Lieutenant **WALKER** realized that his troops were becoming nervous; so, at the crucial moment, he jumped over the wall and called for his troops to follow him, with their bayonets fixed. The Russians were panic-stricken by this sudden appearance and, in spite of the threats of their superior officers, retreated in disorder, with Lieutenant **WALKER** and his troops in pursuit.

This incident led to his being awarded the Victoria Cross, the announcement being made on the June 2, 1858 in the London Gazette. Throughout the Winter of 1854, Lieutenant **WALKER** served in the trenches. On April 21, 1855, he volunteered to lead a party which destroyed a Russian rifle-pit, for which he was mentioned in dispatches and promoted into the East Kent Regiment, known as "The Buffs.".

On the night of June 9th, he was in the trenches when he was wounded by a piece of howitzer shell, and he had to have his right arm amputated the same night.

He was sent home in July and, after six months recuperation, joined the depot at Winchester. The following year, the depot was sent to Ireland. In July 1858, the Buffs were sent to the Ionian Islands, and it was in Corfu, in November, **WALKER** was presented with his Victoria Cross by General Sir George Buller.

Superstition: A well known belief which surfaced during the Crimean War (1853-56) - is that it is bad luck if three soldiers were to light their cigarettes from the same match. The third solider to light from that match was likely to be injured or killed.

The same month, the regiment was sent to India; but, after one year there, **WALKER** and part of the regiment were sent to Canton. During the Chinese War, **WALKER** was present at the capture of Chusan, the Battle of Sinho, the surrender of Peking, and the signing of the peace treaty.

The Buffs returned to England in 1861.

Although they went back to India in 1867, **WALKER** remained in charge of the depot at home; but, in 1871, went to serve in the Sub-Continent. In December 1873, he was appointed to the command of the 45th Regiment (Sherwood Foresters) at Rangoon.

Image below: Memorial for William Kerr V.C.

He returned to England in November 1879. He became a General in February 1893, retired in April that year, and, on the 3rd of June, was appointed a Knight Commander of the Bath. He died at Arlington Rectory, and was buried on July 26, 1902, at Folkestone. (Bio by John "J-Cat" Griffith)

William Alexander KERR V.C: A native of Scotland, William Alexander KERR, received the VC from Major General F.T. Farrell at Belgaum, India on September 4, 1858 for his actions as a lieutenant in the 24th Bombay Native Infantry while serving with The southern Mahratta Irregular Horse of the British Indian Army on July 10, 1857 at Kolapore, British India.

Born in Melrose, Scottish Borders, Scotland, he was commissioned in the British Army as a lieutenant and was sent to British India as part of the 24th Bombay Native Infantry and saw action in the 1857 Indian Mutiny.

He was later promoted to the rank of captain and resigned from the Army in 1860 and returned to England where he became involved in horsemanship. He died in Folkstone, Kent at the age of 87 and is buried in section 24 of the old cemetery.

In addition to the Victoria Cross, he also received the Indian Mutiny Medal (1857-1858) with Central India clasp. His Victoria Cross citation reads: "24th Bombay Native Infantry. Lieutenant William Alexander **KERR**. Date of Act of Bravery, 10th July, 1857.

On the breaking out of a mutiny in the 27th Bombay Native Infantry in July, 1857, a party of the mutineers took

Nature: Slow worms and common lizards can be found in this cemetery basking on the gravestones in the warm sun..

Image below: standard issue CWG - this one showing the Maple Leaf of Canada.

up a position in the stronghold, or paga, near the town of Kolapore, and defended themselves to extremity.

Lieutenant **KERR**, of the Southern Mahratta Irregular Horse, took a prominent share of the attack on the position, and at the moment when its capture was of great public importance, he made a dash at one of the gateways, with some dismounted horsemen, and forced an entrance by breaking down the gate.

The attack was completely successful, and the defenders were either killed, wounded, or captured, a result that may with perfect justice be attributed to Lieutenant KERR's dashing and devoted bravery." (Bio by: William Bjornstad)

THEY GAVE THEIR TODAY: There are 44 **COMMONWEALTH WAR GRAVES** (CWGs) in the old cemetery, 22 of these men are named on the Folkestone War Memorial on the Leas. 95 names mentioned on the Folkestone War Memorial are either buried in family graves in the Folkestone cemetery or are commemorated in the old cemetery and buried elsewhere.

There are 3 Canadian **CWGs** in the old cemetery 1 of which is named on the Folkestone War Memorial. There are 25 Canadians mentioned on the Folkestone War Memorial, 5 of these Canadians are buried in the Fokestone cemetery (1 standard **CWG** and 4 mentioned on family graves).

The standard **CWG** headstone is easily spotted because it stands out from surrounding headstones – this is in part because **CWG** headstones were made of white Portland stone or in later years of Limestone – both high quality and hard wearing stones and partly due to the simple sturdy design of the headstone.

As well as these standard **CWG** headstones there are a number of private commonwealth war graves in this cemetery which are not standard design –

these headstones were provided by choice of the family at the time.

The standard white **CWG** headstone includes basic information; regimental badge, name, rank and regiment, service number, age and date of death – the same design irrespective of rank, race or creed.

The private family **CWGs** sometimes include a little more information – an example is the family headstone for L. Cpl. Harry T Milton of the Buffs (East Kent Regiment) who served in India 1914-1917 and died 23rd January 1918, aged 21 years.

Image above: a lovely butterfly found in this cemetery is the common blue butterfly

The **CWGs**, both standard and private family headstones, are in the care of the Commonwealth War Grave Commission (CWGC) – and are cleaned every other year and if badly deteriorated or damaged the CWGC will replace them. The Cross of Sacrifice standing high above all headstones and memorials, is placed at the Cheriton end of the cemetery, and tells us that there are 40 or more **CWGs** here.

Image below: Often seen basking on warm headstones - the common lizard.

These men, some still boys who had under declared their age, joined the military to serve their country and finally lost their lives after being part of terrible battles during WW1.

The listing of **CWGs** in this cemetery can be found towards the end of this book. A service is held each year in the old cemetery (close to the **MACHINE GUN CORP.** memorial) on 11th November – and each year the words are spoken:

> *"They shall grow not old, as we that are left grow old, Age shall not weary them, nor the years condemn, At the going down of the sun and in the morning, We will remember them"*

One of the **CWGs** is to Private Thomas Frank **COCKS** a member of the Kent Cyclist Battalion - this was an interesting concept and was originally

Image above: An example of a regimental crest on a CWG - This crest is The Buffs.

intended as Mounted Infantry for Home Service, part of the Territorial Force.

The Kent Cyclist Battalion were used as Messengers providing lines of communication to the troops, or as stop gap infantry.

Some battalions were converted to infantry battalions. The 1/1st Battalion is an example of this and they served in India during the Great War.

Nature: The wild British native daffodil, smaller than cultivated varieties and fairly rare, is growing in this cemetery. This wild daffodil is two shades of yellow and across the country it is currently in decline but has been found in our cemetery - most likely because no chemicals are used to control weeds.

CHAPTER 7

TITLED AND EMINENT

NAPOLEON BONAPARTE CONNECTION: there is not much known about Baroness Gwendoline Lister R Poynter **DE CHASSIRON** who died at the young age of 21 years old in 1877, at 5 Albion Villas.

Her memorial was hidden under a tree and covered with ivy and brambles and took a team of volunteers some hours to clear the undergrowth away.

However, this work was worth the effort as research confirmed that Baroness Gwendoline's husband Barron Guy de Chassiron was the great-grandson of Maria Annunziata Carolina Buonaparte (Bonaparte), sister of Napoleon I, Emperor of France no less!

WARTIME MAYOR: Serving a total of 12 years as Folkestones Mayor, Sir Stephen **PENFOLD** was first elected as Mayor in 1888, four of these years were during the war, and he died at the age of 83 years old (buried in sect 18, consecrated).

For 35 years he was an officer in the Volunteer Force and was very well thought of and respected by all – having considerable interest in the National Lifeboat Institution as well as an interest in the education of young people.

Image above: Memorial to Gwendoline De Chassiron.

Stephen **PENFOLD** was also a member of the Temple Lodge Freemasons.

It was in August 1914 when fishing craft and coal carriers came into the harbour carrying the first refugees from Belgium.

In those early days it was the fishing families, on seeing the heart rending and terrible condition of the refugees, who generously held out the hand of friendship and gladly shared their homes and food.

Folkestone soon became the only open door for these people seeking food and protection – and it brought home to Folkestone people, in a dramatic way, the meaning of the war which England was engaged in.

On 24th August a 'Belgian Committee for Refugees' was formed, led by Stephen **PENFOLD** then Mayor of Folkestone, to provide the Belgian refugees with food, clothing, accommodation and work for those able to work.

News: 16,000 Belgian refugees arrived in a single day. It was the largest influx of refugees in British history (www.bbc.co.)

The size of their task can perhaps be more easily understood by considering these statistics: the number of grants to assist persons to meet their living expenses up to February 1919 was 6,580, the total number of meal supplied was 115,000.

Official records from the time estimate 250,000 Belgian refugees came to Britain during WW1. (www.bbc.co.uk)

Sleeping accommodation was provided for 22,180 people, the total number of refugees sent from Folkestone onwards to other towns was 64,500. The number of garments given out to the Belgian refugees amounted to hundreds of thousands.

A tablet in tribute of this work was erected in the Town Hall and the Belgian Vice Consul said:

Image above: Memorial to Stephen Penfold

> *"The Belgians, driven out of their homes, deprived of everything, ruined, flee from their destroyed towns and villages. The sea is free and guides them to their old and trusted protectrice –*

England. The refugees land by thousands, without bread, without clothes, without hope, the soul as suffering as the body. Then, Ladies and Gentlemen, it is here that your work began. Immediately your compassion awakes. The deeper our misery, the more generous your charity, and with this fine business-like spirit which makes the strength of your nation, help is spontaneously organised."

Stephen **PENFOLD** received a knighthood in 1915 for the work he did in receiving the Belgian refugees at Folkestone during the war years. A fine painting by Fredo Franzoni entitled "The Landing Of The Belgian Refugees" is proudly displayed in Foklestones Town Hall.

The Belgian Vice-Consul said: "And in times to come, when the blessings of peace will have blotted out the sufferings and sorrows, their thoughts will go back, with fervent emotion, towards the white coast of England and towards this beautiful town of Folkestone, and they will say - There are our friends".

J.C. Carlile

EDUCATIONALIST: Born in 1805 and left an orphan at an early age Robert William **BOARER** J.P became a significant and well thought of character in Folkestone where he lived the last 16 years of his life.

Throughout his life he took a strong interest in the education of the working class and was closely connected with the management of British Schools. He also felt strongly about the abolition of church rates, which he was actively involved in.

When the new Folkestone cemetery was formed he was elected and served on the Burial Board and in latter years he designed and had constructed his own burial vault. During his time in Folkestone he was elected to the role of Mayor of Folkestone in 1856, 1857 and 1861. Robert **BOARER** remained a councillor until 1863 when he was elected an Alderman, having already been appointed a Justice of the Peace. In 1868 his term of office as Alderman expired, he was re-elected.

However, when Robert **BOARER** put himself forward for the role of Mayor again, there was a discrepancy with the voting and Robert **BOARER** then broke away from the Town council and declined to stand again as an Alderman.

Image below: Memorial to Robert Boarer

Superstition: During the 19th century, across Europe, the deceased were always carried out of the house feet first so they wouldn't look back into the house and beckon to someone else, who would have to go along with them.

Image below: a carved angel with beautiful wings - notice the star symbolising eternity or immortality and divine guidance.

As you walk into the cemetery through the main gates, turn left at the Machine Gun Corps memorial, within yards you will see on your left the memorial to Robert William **BOARER** J.P and atop the tall stone plinth is a statue of an adult with a child reading a book indicating Robert **BOARERS** lifelong interest in education.

MEMBER OF PARLIAMENT: Viscount Charles **MARSHAM** M.P, 3rd Earl of Romney was returned to Parliament as one of two representatives for Kent West in 1841, a seat he held until 1845.

The latter year he succeeded his father in the earldom and took his seat in the House of Lords. For some years Charles **MARSHAM** was Chairman of the Kent Magistrates and presided over the Court of General Sessions and gained respect from peers and colleagues.

He was President of the Marine Society, Governor of Charter House and Chairman of several other institutions and took a very active part in local affairs showing a keen interest in sanitary reform. Such was his detailed understanding of sanitary reform that Government selected him to the Royal Commission for the laws relating to Public Health

SURGEON GENERAL: Born 1848, Sir Arthur Mudge **BRANFOOT** was educated at Epsom College and Guys Hospital, obtaining a first class honours in obstetric medicine. Sir **BRANFOOT** entered the Madras Medical Service as Assistant Surgeon in 1872 and was appointed Civil Surgeon at Cocanada, and afterwards became Resident Surgeon at the General Hospital, Madras until he was appointed as Superintendent of the Government Maternity Hospital in 1879, and in 1881 Professor of Midwifery and Gynaecology at the Madras Medical College.

Further promotion came in 1901 when he was appointed Surgeon-General to the Government of Madras, and for a short time he served as Principal Medical Officer of the Bangalore and Southern Districts.

He retired in 1903 and one year later became President of the Medical Board at the India Office, with the appointment for ten years as Surgeon-General.

The Government Hospital for Women and Children, in Madras was founded in 1844 as the first specialised maternity hospital in India, and probably in Asia.

It started as a small building where barely one hundred births per year were registered but, in 1882, Sir Arthur Mudge **BRANFOOT** founded the present-day buildings which catered for some 18,000 births each year.

This hospital was also the birthplace of the Obstetric and Gynaecological Society of Southern India.

He made a great reputation for himself in Madras, and maintained it in Burma, as one who was ever ready and generous in help given to his fellow-practitioners. It was said of him that:

> *"He was the most distinguished example of an all-round physician and surgeon, capable of dealing well with almost any problem in the whole domain of medicine."*

Image above: This lovely headstone to a 4 year old child features Latin words "post tenebras lux" which means "light after darkness".

Some memorials get damaged as the ground settles and there is not much more to see than an outline of the edging stones, as with the memorial for Sir **BRANFOOT** – but still, these graves are important to the family.

FIERCE LEADER: General Sir Baker Creed **RUSSELL** GCB, KCMG was an Australian born British Army officer who served with distinction in the Indian Mutiny, Anglo-Ashanti War, Anglo-Zulu War and Egyptian War and was appointed Colonel of the 13th Hussars on 20th Jan 1894 with the rank of Major General, promoted to General in 1903.

It was said by his friend Baden-Powell:

A widow in Victorian years was expected to say in mourning for more than two years.

Image above: Memorial for Sir Baker Russell - note the sword being part of the carving.

Superstition: People stopped the clocks in the house at the time of death so they wouldn't have further bad luck.

"Sir Baker RUSSELL was not an orthodox colonel. He was in no way guided by the drill book, and knew little and cared less for the prescribed words of command; but he had a soldiers eye for the country and for where his men ought to be in a fight, and he led them there by his own direction rather than by formal formations as laid down in the book"

On the subject of Sir **RUSSELLS** leadership style Baden-Powell said that Sir Baker was beloved of his men. The regiment, being the 13th Hussars, was nicknamed "The Baker's Dozen."

He practised many things which in those days were looked upon as heresy, but are recognized to-day as producing the highest efficiency, that is, regard for and development of the human side and the individuality of the men themselves.

Sir Baker **RUSSELL** died on 25th Nov 1911 and the funeral was a grand affair and was well reported in local papers:

"The coffin was conveyed to the cemetery on a gun carriage, provided by the Royal Field Artillery from Shorncliffe. It was covered with a large Union Jack, the deceased General's hat and sword and a large cross from Lady Russell . . . the firing party of 100 men was furnished by the Kings Royal Rifles from Shorncliffe.

"The grave was lined with moss and white flowers. The remains were encased in a shell of elm. and the coffin was of polished oak. with massive brass fittings. The plate bore the following inscription:

*"General Sir Baker Creed **RUSSELL**. G.C.8.. K.r.M.G.. died 25th November. 1911, aged 73 years."*

The whole ceremony was of most impressive nature.

CLAN LEADERS: Sir Charles Fitzroy **MACLEAN** (25th Chief of the clan Maclean) lived at West Cliffe House, Folkestone where he died age 86, on 27th December 1883. He was educated at Eton and the Royal Military College at Sandhurst.

He entered the army in the Scots Fusillier Guards in 1816 and received the rank of Colonel in 1846. He was for some time commandant of the 81st Foot and was subsecquently nominated to the post of Military Secretary at Gibralter. Sir Charles was at that time Chief of the Clan **MACLEAN**, succeeded his father in 1847, Major Hector Fitzroy **MACLEAN** was 59 years old when he died at his London residence.

Major Hector was formerly a Major in the Scots Guards, and served in the South African War from 1900-1901 being awarded a medal with four clasps. He also served throughout WW1, gaining two medals. Major Hector Fitzroy **MACLEAN** died 25th July 1932 and is thought to have had a residence at 27 The Leas, Folkestone.

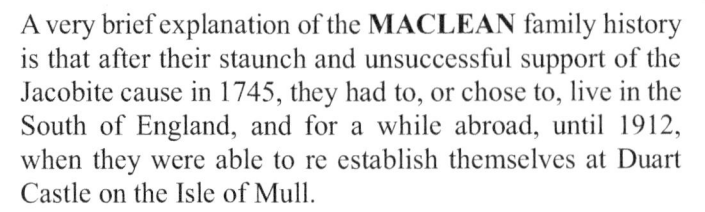

Image above: Maclean family memorial

A very brief explanation of the **MACLEAN** family history is that after their staunch and unsuccessful support of the Jacobite cause in 1745, they had to, or chose to, live in the South of England, and for a while abroad, until 1912, when they were able to re establish themselves at Duart Castle on the Isle of Mull.

The **MACLEANS** are one of the oldest clans in the Highlands – and were involved in clam skirmishes with the Mackinnons, Camerons, MacDonalds and Campbells, as well as the Jacobite risings. In 1936 a centuries old feud between two historic families **MACLEAN** and Campbell was formally ended.

Superstition: If you saw yourself in the mirror of a house where someone had just died, some thought you might also die.

A collection of memorials and gravestones

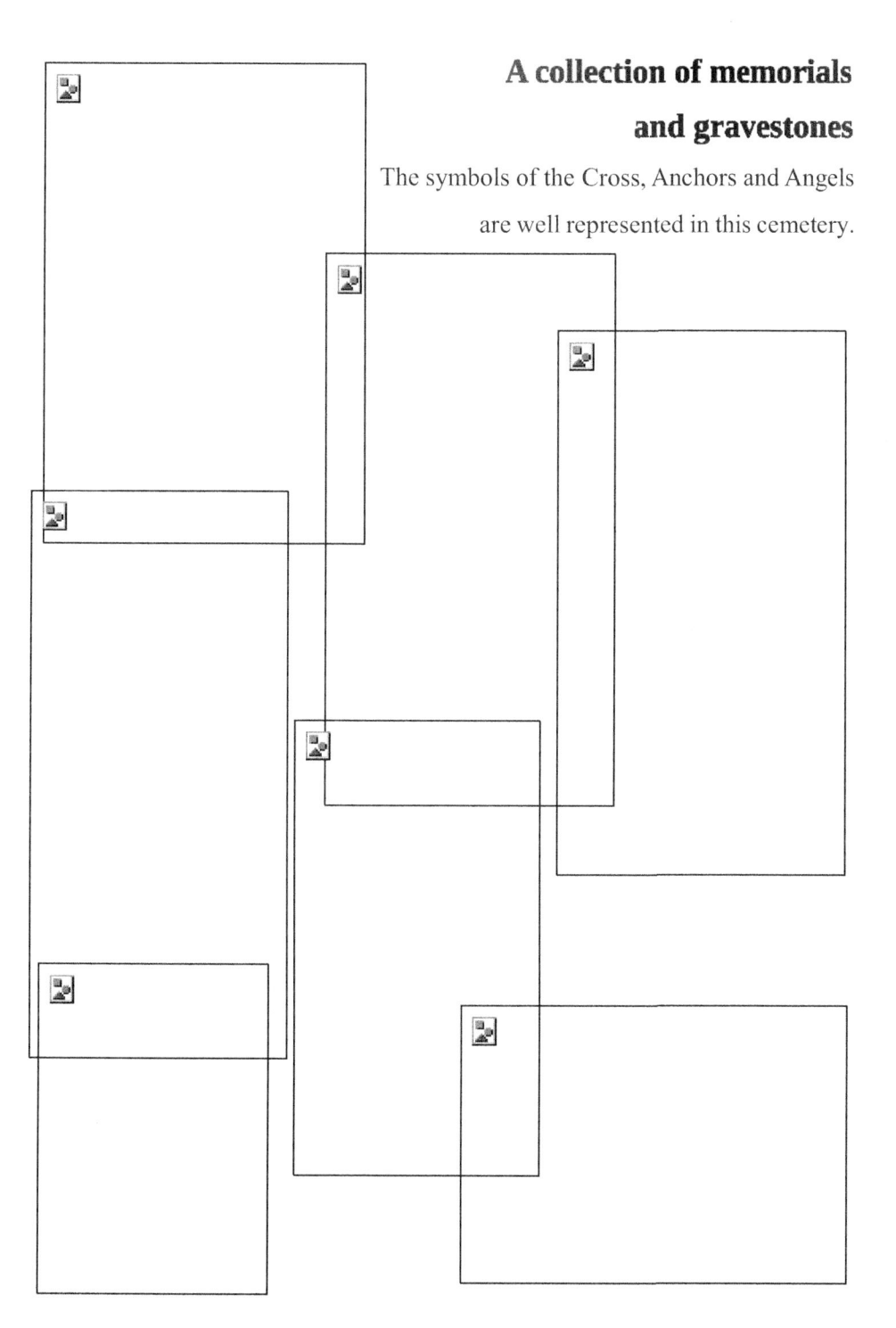

The symbols of the Cross, Anchors and Angels are well represented in this cemetery.

CHAPTER 8

INSANITY AND MYSTERY

RIPPER SUSPECT IN FOLKESTONE: One of the most well known stories of the day (1888) was the story of 'Jack the Ripper' - and for a time it was believed that 'Jack the Ripper' had been spotted applying to enter Elham Union Workhouse.

The 'Jack the Ripper' stories were horrifying and gripped the imagination of Londoners - and across the country too the gruesome stories were followed closely in local papers.

It was October 1888 and a man was seen walking towards Elham Union Workhouse – he appeared to fit the age and description of 'the Ripper' and his trousers and shirt looked as if they were smeared with blood.

He asked to be admitted to the workhouse so that he could receive medical attention for a 'weak heart'- and was detained there whilst his story was checked out. The man had given several names, before admitting to his real name but was later found to have been discharged from the Lancers as 'Unfit for further service' on 8th August 1888 - and so he was released.

Meanwhile in London the real murderer had not struck again since the double murder of Elizabeth Stride and Kate Eddowes and police hoped that these terrible murders had stopped.

Then on 8th November 'The Ripper' struck again with the most savage killing yet. - Mary Jane Kelly had been slaughtered and dismembered.

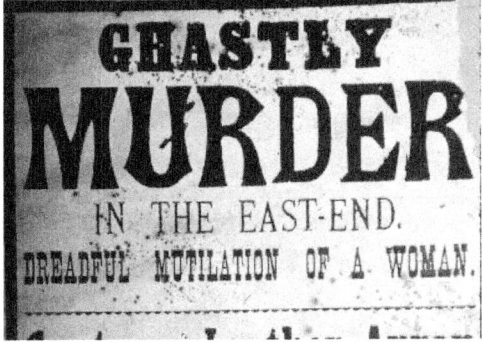

Image above: Ripper headline - The Independent 1888.

Between 1888 and 1891, eleven women were murdered, all sex workers active in the Whitechapel area. The Ripper was accused of killing the eleven women, however, only five can be ascribed to him with any certainty.

Referred to as the 'Canonical Five,' are the five women, who were murdered by the same killer thought to be Jack the Ripper: Mary Ann Nichols, Annie Chapman, Elizabeth Stride, Catherine Eddowes, and Mary Jane Kelly.

A few days later a postcard dated 11th November was sent to Mrs McCarthy (the wife of Mary Jane Kellys landlord) – it had a Folkestone postmark!!

Although wording on the postcard appeared to come from 'The Ripper' because it used stock 'Ripper' words such as 'Dear Boss' and was sign off by 'Jack the Ripper'- it was eventually determined to be a hoax.

Scotland Yard closed the case in 1892, and the identity of 'Jack the Ripper' was never known.

MURDERED ON THE LEAS: A young man named William **SALKELD**, a valet, was walking along the Leas Promenade near the Harvey Memorial with a friend from the Convalescent Home, and with no warning he was suddenly shot in the back – his condition was reported as serious.

A man was quickly arrested for the crime, a gentleman called Augustus Menn. William **SALKELD** was operated on but he died of his wounds the next day. It was reported in the Sheffield Daily Telegraph 16th April 1904:

Image below: Headstone for Willliam Salkeld.

> *"The Folkestone Sensation: Alien Assailant Committed for Murder. At Folkestone yesterday, Auguste Menn, a German subject, was committed for trial charged with the wilful murder of William SALKELD, a valet"*

And *"At Kent Assizes today Augustus Menn (50), German, was charged with the murder of William SALKELD, at Folkestone, on April 7th, The deceased, who was staying at the Convalescent Home, was walking along the sea front when the prisoner shot him in the back with a revolver, death taking place on the following day".*

Both men were strangers – although evidence was produced by **SALKELD'S** companion that Menn had said: *"Doesn't that man look like a bookmaker?"* and others had heard him saying that people often made remarks about him and that if they continued he would shoot them.

Medical evidence was given that Menn was insane, and the jury returned a verdict of wilful murder and he was ordered to be detained during His Majesty's pleasure".

FOUND POISONED ON THE BEACH: On a Sunday night a Hythe fisherman walking between Hythe Gasworks and Coastguard Station discovered Mary Long **ENRIGHT**, an American women lying on the beach partially unconscious.

The fisherman called for help and the women was moved to the Coastguard watch house. The women was wet through and appeared to be suffering from poison. She was given an emetic to cause vomiting, and dry clothes before being taken to the Royal Victorian Hospital in Folkestone.

The women was identified as Mary Long **ENRIGHT** 34 years old, and had been a model employed in a New York ladies mantle shop, but at this time was staying at a boarding house in Bouverie Square.

The House Surgeon determined that she had taken three tablets of mercury chloride, she was almost pulseless and had considerable abdominal pain – and although with treatment she appeared to recover, she died shortly after.

Mary had been in good health, and although her husband had died two years before, did not seem to be overly depressed, but more concerned that she could not get back to America quickly.

At the inquest it was said that the mercury chloride tablets would have been taken deliberately because the taste would be too noxious to have been taken accidentally. The Jury returned a verdict of 'suicide during temporary insanity'.

MYSTERIOUS DEATH OF MAHARAJAH VALET: In 1893 the Maharajah of Bhownnuggar visited England and for a few days he was a guest of the Prince of Wales in London.

Superstition:: Clocks would be stopped to mark the time of death. It was thought that if the clocks were not stopped then time would continue and allow the spirits to remain in the present to haunt or endlessly roam between states of existence. Once the deceased was laid to rest then clocks could be uncovered and restarted.

Image below: a lovely larger than life-size angel stone carving

On leaving London he was to spend a week in Folkestone before embarking for the Continent. Once arriving in Folkestone his valet Rajabhai **SHERBHAI**, a Sepoy of 40 years old, went missing. It was said that he was suffering with 'guinea worm' and in some pain, and was in low spirits'.

His turban was found on the beach the next morning by George a coast guardsman and a few days after his body was found on the foreshore by a lamplighter named Gregory.

Nature: A butterfly frequently seen along the south east coast, or where there is buddleia growing - is the Comma, colours - a deep orangy brown with black markings.

He still had small items of value on him and there was no evidence of violence. It was determined by the Jury that there was no evidence to show how he came by his death, which was caused by drowning.

TRAGIC HONEYMOON DEATH: It was February 1905 and Major Harry Francis **PAKENHAM** and his new bride May had travelled to Folkestone from Knightsbridge where their marriage had taken place.

Major **PAKENHAM** and May stayed at the Royal Pavilion Hotel for their honeymoon – and in the evening Major **PAKENHAM** who seemed in good spirits said he would take a short stroll, telling his new wife that he wouldn't be too long.

And that was the last he was seen alive – following his disappearance a boatman picked up an overcoat near Folkestone Harbour which was identified as belonging to the Major and in the pocket there was a handkerchief bearing his name and a note which included the words *"cannot stand this awful strain, must end it"* - the note went on to say he saw no prospect of getting better.

The Majors body was found just after 4am on the seashore close to the spot where the overcoat was found.

During the Victorian years men could continue working after a loved one died, but women were expected to be isolated at home.

Major **PAKENHAM** had suffered with enteric fever which he had contracted when he served in the Kings Royal Rifles. in South Africa. A verdict of *'Suicide whilst temporarily insane'* was given.

EVIDENCE OF LACERATIONS: Gertrude Fanny **FLETCHER** lived with her husband Mr John Fletcher, a grocer, at an address in Holloway Road, London – but as she was native of Folkestone her body was brought to Folkestone for burial.

Gertrude had died shortly after giving birth and although the body was examined at the request of her husband Mr Fletcher, he had then allowed his wife to be buried. At the request of the Home Secretary the body was exhumed and it was referred to the Coroner for a post mortem to be carried out.

A nurse gave evidence about Doctor W, who had attended the birth, and said he seemed to be clumsy when using the instruments and she thought that he may have just recovered from a bout of drunkenness.

Doctor W had sent for another doctor, and then another doctor was called in – shortly after that the baby was born. Gertrude **FLETCHER** was in a critical state and a Harley Street doctor was consulted who advised she needed an urgent operation in the morning – however Gertrude died that night.

Image above: On instruction from the Home Office the body was exhumed.

The Coroner described terrible lacerations to her internal organs caused by surgical instruments and said death had been caused by shock and exhaustion caused by these injuries.

Doctor W was charged with manslaughter through gross and culpable negligence.

COLONEL FOUND SHOT: Living in Grimston Avenue, 65 year old Colonel Edward William **FLEMING** who had served in the Royal Artillery, but was now retired, had been receiving treatment for a nervous breakdown. But on this morning of May 1913 about 11 am he went out for a walk, seemingly in good spirits.

He had gone into the lavatory under the Town Hall, the lavatory attendant had noticed that the Colonel was acting

Middle class families often took outings to these garden cemeteries on weekends – sometimes having family picnics in the cemetery.

Superstition: During the 19th century the deceased was always carried out of the house feet first so they wouldn't look back into the house and beckon to someone else, who would have to go along with them.

Alternatively it was thought that if the body was carried out head first, the deceased could see where the house was and return to haunt it.

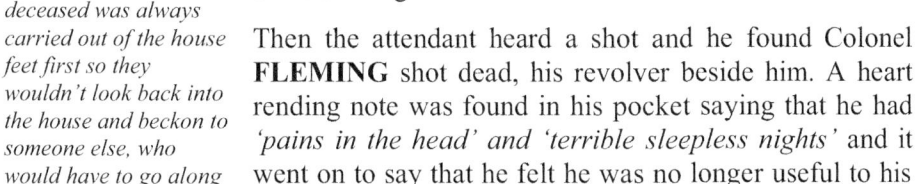

Image above: A common lizard basking in the warm sunlight on a headstone

strangely as he seemed to change his mind and go out, but came back again.

Then the attendant heard a shot and he found Colonel **FLEMING** shot dead, his revolver beside him. A heart rending note was found in his pocket saying that he had *'pains in the head' and 'terrible sleepless nights'* and it went on to say that he felt he was no longer useful to his family.

At his inquest his son said that his father imagined himself to be nearly bankrupt, although he was in fact quite wealthy. The Coroners verdict was *'Suicide during temporary insanity'*.

DEATH OF A CYCLIST: Living with his mother in Bouverie Square, Frederick Lemuel **WALL** was a well known Kentish cyclist and champion hill climber. According to his mother Frederick WALL had left home on 15th April to cycle to Upper Norwood, with the intention of returning the following Thursday.

However he did not return as he said he would and his mother, being concerned, wrote to the address in Upper Norwood. A few days later the letter was returned marked 'Not Known'

The door of Fredericks room was locked, which was not unusual when he went away – but his mother was by now very worried and decided to get the room broken into.

She found Fredericks body in bed in an advanced state of decomposition. The attending doctor said that death had taken place four weeks ago.

Besides the lock on the door it was also secured with two bolts. The bike that Frederick would have taken with him was also standing in the room.

The mystery was that no one had seen Frederick **WALL** return from his journey and the window was still fastened from the inside. Due to the advanced state of decomposition the doctor said a post mortem would be pointless and the Jury gave a verdict of *'Found Dead'*.

MYSTERY INJURIES: It was the habit of 23 year old Ada **HONEYBOURNE** to work as 'general help' or 'charing' for local people and on this occasion she went out to one of her weekly jobs. Later in the day her cleaning client Mrs Pursey told Ada's mother that Ada had somehow injured herself and been taken to hospital. Ada complained of her 'poor back and her poor head' but could not recall how she came about her injuries. Mrs Pursey thought that Ada may have fallen from a window - but nobody had heard or seen her fall.

Image below: cemetery view

Ada had bruising and cuts over her right ear and bruises to different parts of her body and although the doctor attended daily, Ada lapsed into a coma, getting weaker until she died shortly after (1905).

The inquest jury decided that 'the deceased died from concussion of the brain, but how it was caused there was no evidence to show'.

HEADLESS BODY OF CHILD FOUND: The decapitated body of 8 month Phyllis Annie **O'NEALE** (1915) was found next to the railway line (between Junction and Harbour stations) - but despite a search the childs head could not be found.

Mrs O'Neal, the mother had been living, on and off, with a soldier from Shorncliffe Camp who paid her rent and she said she had left her child with her sister whilst she looked for new lodgings and work.

At the trial Dr Lidderdale said that the decapitation had not been done by a train, but looked as if it had been done by somebody who knew what they were doing. A witness said that Mrs O'Neal had been seen carrying a small brown paper parcel up to her room and then later came down for a cup of tea.

In court Inspector Lawrence dramatically produced the childs head which he had found in the mothers bed - the mother almost fainted. At the Inquest however, quite suddenly, Mrs O'Neale confessed "Yes I did do it, I am sorry I did do it". Mrs O'Neal was charged with wilfully murdering her 8 month old child.

Superstition: When a family member died, it was tradition to close the curtains and cover all mirrors so that the deceased's image didn't get trapped in the looking glass.

There are many beautiful memorials in the old cemetery - this is a fine example

CHAPTER 9
CREATIVE AND ARTISTIC

MEZZOTINT ENGRAVER: John Edwin **PORTER** described as an 'artist and drawing master' who died in 1878 was a renown Mezzotint Engraver, his studio was in Cheriton Place.

The **PORTER** family were not given to much socialising being very much focused on their families – so there is little known about John **PORTERS** personal life.

However there are many of his engravings, which were generally portraits, hanging in the National Gallery.

LANDSCAPE ARTIST: John James **WILSON** was born in Lambeth, London around 1818, where he was also baptised in 1833. John James married Elizabeth Parker in 1845 and started his family with the birth of his daughter Elizabeth Parker Wilson in the same year.

The family at that time lived near Gravesend, Kent. According to the 1861 census, the WILSON family were now living at 3 West Terrace Folkestone, Kent – and more children were added to the family; William, Frank, Amy and Vernon all born in Folkestone.

Although by then there is no mention of his first child Elizabeth - but as years pass yet more children are added to the family (and at least one child had died) which are by now living at Belle Vue House, Folkestone.

John James **WILSON** exhibited his paintings at the main galleries and societies throughout the British Isles including the Royal Academy of Arts (55 paintings), the British Institution (57 paintings), Royal Society of British

Image above: Headstone for John Porter.

The Latin phrase Memento mori means 'remember you must die'.

Image above: Headstone for John Wilson.

Artists (384 paintings), the Royal Scottish Academy (106 paintings), Royal Glasgow Institute of the Fine Arts (3 paintings), and the Royal Hibernian Academy (14 paintings). He exhibited his first painting (Cottages near Southampton) at the British Institution in 1834.

At the age of around 28, the quality of John James **WILSON**'S work was recognised when he was elected a member of the RBA in 1845.

Many of his seascapes featured locations around the English Channel. In 1875, the year of his death, three paintings submitted by his widow (The old 'Star' Newington, Kent; On the coast, Etretat, Normandy; Trawler going out- Normandy) were exhibited at the Royal Society of British Artists.

These and his other paintings are still popular and are sold at auction rooms around the UK and elsewhere. The enduring popularity of John James **WILSON'S** paintings is evident in that prints and painted copies of his works are still readily available, and eighteen of his paintings are distributed in public art collections throughout the UK.

TRANSFORMED BRITISH LITERATURE:

Catherine **CROWE** was a respected novelist and cultural celebrity in the mid-nineteenth century and was one of seven amazing women writers who transformed British Literature according to author Shelley De Wees.

Superstition: It was thought that mirrors could trap the deceased person, so all the mirrors in the house would be covered in black cloth. Often, family photos and paintings would also be turned upside or turned to face the wall.

CROWE spent most of her childhood years, and was educated, in Kent. She married an army officer, Major John Crowe (1783–1860) and they had a son but she was unhappy in her marriage .

By 1838 she was separated from her husband and living in Edinburgh where she had met several other writers, in London too she met writers of renown, Harriet Martineau and William Makepeace Thackeray.

CROWE's two plays, the verse tragedy 'Cristodemus' (1838) and the melodrama 'The Cruel Kindness'(1853) both had historical themes paralleling her own family problems.

Poisonous yew trees were planted in churchyards so that farmers could ensure that their animals didn't stray into them.

The book that established **CROWE** as a novelist was 'The Adventures of Susan Hopley' (1841), followed by 'Men and Women' (1844) and the well-received 'The Story of Lily Dawson'(1847), The 'Adventures of a Beauty' (1852), and 'Linny Lockwood' (1854).

Though set in middle-class life, her stories had complicated, sensational plots, whilst also commenting on the predicaments of Victorian women brought up in seclusion to be mistreated by those men who did not subscribe to standards of decent behaviour.

The 'Vicissitudes of a Servant Girl' adapted from CROWEs' novel by George Dibdin Pitt, opened at the Royal Victoria Theatre in 1841 and became a long-running success and by 1849 had been performed 343 times.

Catherine **CROWE** turned increasingly to supernatural subjects, inspired by German writers. Her collection 'The Night-side of Nature' (1848) became her most popular work and was translated into German and French, and is said to have influenced the views of Charles Baudelaire.

Another type of memento mori was a lock of the deceased's hair, which was arranged artfully and preserved in a locket.

In February 1854 she was discovered naked in Edinburgh one night, convinced that spirits had rendered her invisible - she was treated for mental illness and recovered.

Two of her ghost stories reappeared in 'Victorian Ghost Stories' (1936). Catherine **CROWE** also wrote a number of books for children, including 'Pippie's Warning' or, 'Mind Your Temper'(1848), 'The Story of Arthur Hunter and his First Shilling' (1861) and 'The Adventures of a Monkey'(1862).

From 1852 onwards she lived in London and abroad but moved to Folkestone in 1871 where she died the following year.

Image above: Gravestone for Catherine Crowe

Image above: Memorial for Bithia Mary Croker

Superstition: It was thought that If you hear a clap of thunder following a burial it indicates that the soul of the departed has reached heaven

PROLIFIC LITERARY CAREER: Bithia Mary **CROKER** was an Irish novelist, most of her work was about life and society in British India.

Her 1917 novel 'The Road to Mandalay' set in Burma, was the uncredited basis for a 1926 American silent film, of which only excerpts survive.

She was also a notable writer of ghost stories. **CROKER's** prolific literary career spanned 37 years, from 1882 when she was 33 years old, until 1919. She wrote 44 novels and six volumes of short stories.

It is said that during a heated debate in the House of Commons Mr Gladstone was seen reading 'Popular Pride' - and this certainly may have helped to promote the book more widely.

On her death it was reported that she was very well known in literary circles and after more than 30 years of novel writing she had still retained a very firm hold on the affections of the novel reading public.

Fourteen years spent in India and Burma had given her time and the material for some of her best works, including 'In Old Madras' and two other recent books 'Blue China' and a volume of short stories entitled 'Odds and Ends'.

Although Bithia Mary **CROKER** lived at 5 Radnor Cliff, she was in a London nursing home when she died unexpectedly – only weeks after signing a contract with her publishers for her next three books. Bithia Mary **CROKER** was buried in Folkestone cemetery close to her husbands grave.

FOSSIL COLLECTOR: THE death was announced in 'Nature' publication of Mr. John **GRIFFITHS** who was a well-known fossil-collector, aged 62 at death.

He was born in Dover but at time of death lived at 8 Folly Cottages, Folkestone. John **GRIFFITHS** rendered important service to a number of well known researchers in their understanding on the Gault and associated formations, and he discovered a large proportion of the most important Gault fossils now in the British Museum and the Museum of Practical Geology.

Is is said the John **GRIFFITHS** spent much of his time, both summer and winter at The Warren, observing nature and what he did not know was not worth knowing - and his knowledge of 'Little Switzerland' was unique.

When asked about the future of the Warren he said:

"As sure as tomorrows sun will rise so sure will there be someday a great collapse of cliff and land somewhere between Martello and Abbots Cliff tunnels".

It was announced in the Geological Magazine that John **GRIFFITHS** suffered from being permanently disabled by rheumatism but that Folkestone townspeople helped raise funds for his keep.

Around 1865 John **GRIFFITHS** found some dinosaurian remains, including osteoderms, at the shoreline near Folkestone in Kent, which he sold to the metallurgist Dr. John Percy.

Dr Percy brought them to the attention of Thomas Henry Huxley, who paid **GRIFFITHS** to dig up all fossils he could find at the site. Despite being hampered by the fact that it was located between the tidemarks, he managed to uncover several additional bones and parts of the body armour.

John **GRIFFITHS** was described as one of Folkestones 'grand old men' - humble and unassuming, a perfect gentleman - he died in 1911.

It was common to take a photographs of the deceased as the remembrance, especially babies and children, and often pupils were painted over the closed eyelids to that the eyes looked open.

Image above, Gravestone shaped like a fossil for John Griffiths

Image below: Memorial for William Clauson-Theu

PIONEER OF CODE: William **CLAUSON-THEU** who died 1807 was the pioneer of Telegraphic Coding and author of the A.B.C and other Codes.

His book, the 'A.B.C. of Wireless Telegraphy', had at least five reprints and is still in publication, albeit as a 'classic' work only for reference.

It seems William grew up and worked as a Shipping Agent and during this period he used his spare time to address the problems of ship to shore communications via wireless telegraphy.

He published his first work; the 'A.B.C. of Wireless Telegraphy' in 1883. Both he, and his twin brother Henry married, what appears to have been two sisters Charlotte & Eliza Dixon respectively.

William & Charlotte had two daughters; Edith, (Born 1864) and Florence (Born 1866); and once they were grown up they also began to help their father in his later work regarding the telegraphy including the 'A1 Code'.

He lived until 1907 and died nearly a year after the death of his wife, following a bout of influenza. He was a Freeman of the Glaziers Company of the City of London, a P.M. of two Masonic Lodges and was well known as a generous contributor to religious, philanthropic, and social objects. Her Majesty, Queen Victoria, and King (Edward VII), graciously accepted copies of the "A1 Code".

Superstition: It was thought to be bad luck to meet a funeral procession head on. If you see one approaching, turn around. If this is unavoidable, hold on to a button until the funeral cortege passes

In his later years, Mr William **CLAUSON-THEU** resided at Folkestone and his funeral took place at the Folkestone Cemetery 22 February 1907. His coffin was laid in a vault, where rested the remains of the deceased gentleman's wife. The coffin was of polished oak, and bore the inscription:

*"William **CLAUSON-THEU**: Died 15 February, 1907, Aged 73 Years".*

CHAPTER 10
THE END, OR IS

THE SMALL 'Friends of old Folkestone cemetery' volunteer group get together to work in the old cemetery every Saturday – some 'Friends' come weekly, some less frequently – but always welcome.

These people have been an absolute delight and inspiration to work with. We chat about what we may have found this time and find it endlessly fascinating as we piece together bit by bit the different aspects of Folkestone and surrounding villages through the Victorian years which our research uncovers.

The characters included in this book are the result of researching just some of the memorials or headstones we have uncovered whilst working there, there are many more to discover.

In considering how this book would be formatted – I decided that I should present the information about each person set in an abbreviated form of historical context – because then (I thought) it would be possible to gain some understanding of the wider picture of how and why Folkestone became the town and place that it is now.

I hope the structure I have given this book has made some sense for you the reader.

In putting together brief descriptions of the people who once lived in Folkestone for this book, more and more I realise that everyone has their story. Its not only the 'eminent or titled' although we have those people in this cemetery too – far from it - each person no matter what

Image above: A handsome memorial incorporating the anchor set on rocks - a Christian symbol of hope or representing life as a sailor.

Image above: A stone carving of a lady looking sadly to heaven, with an anchor under her hand

Superstition: It was thought that a person could not die on a mattress with feathers of wild fowl, so when someone was dying a slow death, the person would sometimes be carried to a different mattress to ease the suffering.

their station in life contributed to Folkestone being the unique and wonderful place that it is now.

Each little story whilst not telling you the complete life of each person – still, I hope gives a sense of the life and times that these people lived through.

This account includes more than 150 names - and I know that there are many more interesting characters to find out about - perhaps another book another time.

For myself, I have not lived by the sea all my life, I came here almost two decades ago and I now never want to move away from the sea – it is unbelievably beautiful and awesomely frightening all at once.

And as a bonus I find it almost impossible to get lost now because I can orientate myself according to where the coastline is.

However, more seriously the more I have researched for this book the more respect I have for Folkestones fishing community and heritage – those men and boys whose livelihood depended on the sea - and for some it still does.

These people had to be tough to survive the storms and other dangers at sea and their families would have needed to be stoic and resilient in the face of loss, with community coming together to support each other when necessary.

It is often thought that out of chaos comes order – it is a pattern we can see through the Victorian years and you will perhaps see it all around you now too. Change rarely comes from tranquillity and calmness, most always from chaos and unrest.

I think that core of grit and toughness which is evidenced throughout the Victorian years, especially in the fishing community, is clearly evident in born and bred Folkestone people who want nothing more than to see Folkestone and the surrounding area becoming once again a vibrant, prosperous and attractive place to live and work - in a beautiful natural setting of hills and valleys, edged by the sea.

Symbolism: The hourglass is a symbol of limited time on earth.

Image to the left: a stone carving cherub

Note: *Throughout this account more than 150 characters have been named (family name in* **bold** *font), or alluded to, who are buried in the old cemetery.*

To find out exactly where each grave is - see the listing of names, sections and plot numbers on the following pages - and refer to page 14 for a plan of the cemetery.

ABOUT FOFC

For readers who are interested and may wish to join our working group on Saturday mornings or, if not to work, perhaps would like to follow our progress here is some information.

Volunteer Group: Friends of old Folkestone cemetery
Web: www.fofc.uk
FB: Friends of old Folkestone cemetery.
Work sessions: Saturday 10.30 am to 1.30 pm
Email: admin@fofc.uk

Burial Authority: Folkestone & Hythe District Council
Tel: 01303 853000
Web: www.folkestone-hythe.gov.uk

Image to left Remembrance Day unveiling of Interpretation Panel by Mayor of Folkestone Ann Berry and Chairman of F&HDC David Owen.

CWG BURIAL PLOTS

NAME	SECT	PLOT	NAMES	SECT	PLOT
Ames, A.R.	20	1963 c	Millen, L.F.	7	412 u
Barron, L.	17	466 c	Milton, H.T.	20	1926 c
Blackford, H.	11	2025 u	Mochrie, J.S.	7	411 u
Campbell, J.E.	26	5430 c	Noyes, C.H.C.	17	441 c
Champion, A.	20	1885 c	Ollivant, A.H.	18	986 c
Cocks, T.F.	7	100 u	Oxford, C.J.	11	2105 u
Cullen, J.A.	16	158 c	Page, W.H.	26	5276 c
Curtis, A.R.	14	2603 u	Parkes, G.C.C.	20	1951 c
Dilnot, L.H.	20	1775 c	Patterson, W.E.W.	14	2296 u
Ellender, R.H.	7	281 u	Robus, P.J.	20	1834 c
Ellis, A.V.	7	320 u	Sackree, A.	14	2309 u
Finn, F.W.	20	1961 c	Sackville-West, K.F.	14	2307 u
Goff, R.W.	17	375 c	Shipp, H.	7	52 u
Grace, W.G.	16	12 c	Solomon, R.	20	1712 c
Harris, W.J.	4	3157 u	Standing, G.T.	2	6841 c
Haydon, T.	2	6834 c	Steels, T.E.J.	16	87 c
Heydon, G.W.C.	4	3569 u	Taylor, F.J.	16	88 c
Holliday, T.	20	1804 c	Tiddy, J.	25	4472 c
Jordon, R.	11	2089 u	Tull, W.S.P.	7	434 u
Kingsbury, J.H.	24	3937 c	Upton, W.G.	25	4369 c
Mant, W.J.J.	7	95 u	Welsh, F.A.M.	5	3898 c
Marshall, F.	7	321 u	Wright, L.C.	20	1971 c

u - unconsecrated | c - consecrated

VICTORIA CROSS RECIPIENTS

NAMES	SECT	PLOT
Commerell, J.E.	22	3237 c
Kerr, W.A.	24	3911 c
Walker, M.	18	1259 c

AIR RAID VICTIMS BURIAL PLOTS

NAME   SECT / PLOT

NAME	SECT	PLOT
NORRIS, Florence, Florence and William	2	6783
BEER, Annie and Annie Rosie	2	6805a
BEER, William and Arthur	2	6805b
HAYES, Martha	3	8504
WILSON, Isabella	3	8687
HAMBLY, Johannah	3	8720
STOKES, Frederick	4	3140
BUTCHER, George	7	68
DAY, Frederick	7	335
GRIMES, Edith	7	338
HARRISON, Fanny	7	339
BURKE, John	7	340
FRANCIS, Florence	7	386
HUGHES, Rose	7	409
WAUGH, Elizabeth	7	431
LAXTON, Katherine	7	475
HOLLOWAY, Mary	8	1067
HOLLOWAY, Veronica	8	1068
COOPER, Phyllis	13	2765
MAXTED, Louisa	20	1700
DICKER, Sarah and Edith	20	1702

AIR RAID VICTIMS BURIAL PLOTS

NAME	SECT	PLOT
HALL, William	20	1705
BARTLEET, Maggie	20	1852
GRAVES, Richard	20	1854
BROCKWAY, Sydney	20	1855
BURVILLE, Hilda	20	1856
REED, Mabel	20	1857
TERRY, Gwendoline	20	1858
JACKMAN, Dorothy	20	1859
RUMSEY, Florrie	20	1862
EALES, Edith	20	1863
HARRIS, Caroline	20	1864
CASTLE, Albert	20	1866
HAMBROOK, Ethel	20	1867
BARKER, Eliza	20	1870
GOULD, Edward	20	1871
BANKS, Harold	20	1872
CLARK, William	20	1873
MACDONALD, Agnes	20	1874
HAYWARD, Louisa	21	2758
ROBINSON, John (Jackie)	29	5787
HAYES, Dennis	29	7790
MCGUIRE, Ernie	29	5764

BURIAL PLOTS (NAMED)

NAME	SECT / PLOT	PAGE NO.
MOSS, Lily	26 5562a	4 & 16
CHAPMAN, Clara	26 5562b	4
BUXTON, baby	plot unknown	4
KNIGHT, Lillian	plot unknown	4
NEALE, Phyllis	28 5193	4
CLARKE, James Payne	14 2503	15
DALY, Timothy	5 3819	16
HOLLIDAY, William George	17 627	18
O'BRIEN, Herbert	5 3909	19
COOK, William (Cookie)	7 674	21 & 40
WILLS, William Brice	7 367	22
WARMAN, Stephen	20 1793	23
COOK, Stephen	4 3580	25
WATKIN, Alfred	24 3921	27
TITE family	18 1322	28
BRICE, Edward	3 8219	28
HALL, Benjamin	23 3815	28
HINKLEY, William	3 8054	28
BECKINGHAM, Henry	4 3532	29
MITCHELL, William	14 2499	29
PEDEN, George	30 3041	30
DENHAM, Harold	23 3801	30
WEATHERHEAD, Robert	2 7356	31, 50 & 52
ANDERSON, John	3 8439	31
HORN, William and Ann	9 1237	32
SPOOR, Ralph	14 2537	33
WESTON, Sydney	15 2612	39
MONSELL, Harriett *	26 5337	41
CLEWER NUNS, Emma, Marion, Ethelreda * close by		41
DAWSON, Arthur	26 5336	42
RAMELL, Thomas	5 3637	42
JOY, Charlie	9 1028	42
PECHEY, Edith	18 1256	43
GROSSER KURFURST	26	44
SAUNDERS, William	4 3202	45

BURIAL PLOTS (NAMED)

NAME	SECT / PLOT	PAGE NO.
COPPING, Herbert	7 548	50
HALL, Stephen	23 3727	50
FRODSHAM, William	2 7079	50
HART, John	plot unknown	50
FAGG, Edward	11 2017	50
MARSHALL, William	4 3130	50
CORRIE, John	3 8751	51
PHILPOTT, David	3 8606	52
FREEMAN, Robert	24 4029	52
FAGG, Robert	3 8654	52
WILLIAMS, Nicholas	11 2079	52
DECK, Phyllis	16 18	53
MACHINE GUN CORP	close to main entrance	54
DE CHASSIRON, Gwendoline	26 5909	61
PENFOLD, Stephen	18 890	61
BOARER, Robert	30 3028	63
MARSHAM, Charles	26 5439	64
BRANFOOT, Arthur	18 1039	64
RUSSELL, Baker Creed	18 1021	65
MACLEAN, Charles	22 2891	67
SALKELD, William	3 8477	70
ENRIGHT, Mary	7 105	71
SHERBHAI, Rajabhai	10 1704	72
PAKENHAM, Harry	18 1082	72
FLETCHER, Gertrude	18 859	73
FLEMMING, Edward	24 3960	73
WALL, Frederick	14 2558	74
HONEYBOURNE, Ada	3 8544	75
NEALE, Phyllis	28 5193	75
PORTER, John	30 3063	77
WILSON, John	17 809	77
CROWE, Catherine	17 718	78
CROKER, Mary	14 2314	80
GRIFFITHS, John	5 3896	80
CLAUSON-THEU, William	14 2435	82

SOURCES AND FURTHER READING

Black, R., *Scandal Salvation and Suffrage*, (Matador, an imprint of Troubador Publishing Ltd, 2015)

Brundage, A., *The English Poor Laws, 1700-1930*, (Palgrave, 2002)

Editors of the 'Poor Law Officers Journal', *The Law Relating To The Relief Of The Poor*, (The Poor-Law Publications Company, 1912)

Easdown, M., Genth, T., *A Glint In The Sky,* (Pen & Sword Military Books, 2004)

Easdown, E. & Rooney, E., *More Tales From The Tap Room,* (A.R. Adams & Sons, 2004)

Easdown, M., Sage, L., *Foul Deeds & Suspicious Deaths Around Folkestone & Dover* (Wharncliffe Books, 2006)

English, J., *English's Reminiscences of Old Folkestone Smugglers and Smuggling Days, Scholars Choice* (F. J. Parsons, Ltd, Folkestone)

Halliday, S., (The History Press, 2011)

Higginbotham, P., *The Workhouse Cookbook,* (The History Press, 2016)

Higginbotham, P., *The Workhouse Encyclopedia,* (The History Press, 2014)

May, T., *The Victorian Workhouse,* (Shire Library)

May, T., *The Victorian Undertaker*, (Shire Library)

Harrison, W. H., *The Fossil Bride and Other Verses* (out of print)

Platt, R., *Smuggling in the British Isles*, (The History Press, 2011)

Rene-Martin, L., *Sandgate - Rise and Progress of a Village*, (Rene-Martin, L. 2004)

Rutherford, S., *The Victorian Cemetery* (Shire Library, 2008)

Taylor, A. F., *Folkestone - A Third Selection,* (Alan Sutton Publishing Ltd, 1995)

Newspapers:

Folkestone Express, Sandgate, Shorncliffe & Hythe Advertiser

Folkestone, Hythe, Sandgate & Cheriton Herald

Kentish Gazette

Kent & Sussex Courier

Websites:

Ancestry www.ancestry.co.uk

British Newspaper Archive www.britishnewspaperarchive.co.uk/

Cook Families Folkestone www.leshaigh.co.uk/folkestone/cookinfo.html

Parish Workhouses www.workhouses.org.uk/parishes/

The Rescue of the Crew of the Benvenue: www.leshaigh.co.uk/folkestone/benvenue.html

Printed in Great Britain
by Amazon